Hairdressing: Level 3

The Interactive Textbook

An Interactive Multimedia
Blended eLearning System

ATT Training
World leader in multimedia blended eLearning

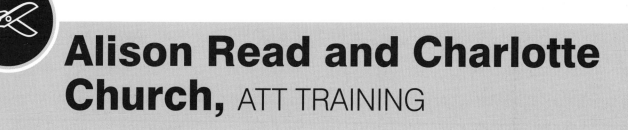

Alison Read and Charlotte Church, ATT TRAINING

Routledge
Taylor & Francis Group

LONDON AND NEW YORK

First published 2013
by Routledge
2 Park Square, Milton Park, Abingdon, Oxon OX14 4RN

Simultaneously published in the USA and Canada
by Routledge
711 Third Avenue, New York, NY 10017

Routledge is an imprint of the Taylor & Francis Group, an informa business

British Library Cataloguing in Publication Data
A catalogue record for this book is available from the British Library

Library of Congress Cataloging in Publication Data
Read, Alison, 1974-
Hairdressing. Level 3 : the interactive textbook / by Alison Read and Charlotte Church.
    p. cm.
    Includes index.
    ISBN 978-0-415-52868-9 (alk. paper) — ISBN 978-0-203-10691-4 1. Hairdressing—
    Textbooks. I. Church, Charlotte, 1981- II. Title.
    TT972.R4237 2012
    646.7'24—dc23
                                                                            2012013651

ISBN: 978-0-415-52868-9 (pbk)
ISBN: 978-0-203-10691-4 (ebk)

Typeset in Helvetica
by RefineCatch Limited, Bungay, Suffolk

Contents

Preface

All of us at ATT Training are proud to be producing the best multimedia blended eLearning materials available for hairdressing training. We have achieved this by working with the best hairdressers, product manufacturers and salons, as well as great colleges and training centres. We started this about fifteen years ago and our materials have got better every year since!

To keep improving, as well as continuing to develop our computer based and online learning materials, we are very pleased to have teamed up with a leading publisher to produce this full-colour and interactive textbook. It can be used on its own or in conjunction with our multimedia materials online. All the essential materials are free for students and even more is available to teachers for a very low annual fee. Please contact us for details: info@atthairdressing.com

This book is the third in the 'Hairdressing: Multimedia Blended eLearning' series:

- Hairdressing – Level 1
- Hairdressing – Level 2
- Hairdressing – Level 3

We hope you find the content useful and informative. Comments, suggestions and feedback are always welcome at our website: www.atthairdressing.com. You will also find links to lots of free online resources to help with your studies.

We also have interesting and useful materials and ideas on these sites; come and join in:

 Facebook: www.facebook.com/atthairdressing

 Twitter: www.twitter.com/atthairdressing

 YouTube: www.youtube.com/atthairdressing

Flickr: www.flickr.com/atthairdressing

Acknowledgements

ATT Training is grateful to the following companies and individuals for supplying assistance and/or materials and working to help with the production of our books and computer based materials:

- Kennadys, Ingatestone, Essex (Salon of the Year winner) www.kennadys.co.uk
- Splinters, London www.splintersacademy.com
- Inter Training Service (ITS)
- Bexley College
- The Manchester College
- Wella
- L'Oréal
- Sandra Brock (consultant)
- John Cornell (photographer)
- Beth Denton
- Shutterstock

Pronunciation of useful words

There are quite a few unusual words and phrases that we come across as hairdressers. In this short section we have listed as many as we can think of – please let us know via the website if you find any more.

To keep it simple we have not used complicated and unusual characters so our method is not perfect, but it is very close. The word is shown followed by the same word spelt phonetically (fon-et-ik-a-lee). A quick tip is that a single vowel like **-o-** is sounded as in 'lock' or if it is shown as **-oh-** then it is said as in 'broke' and if shown as **-oo-** it is sounded as in 'food'.

If you have access to all our online multimedia screens you can listen to how our narrator says the words – he gets most of them right!

Abrasion	(a-bray-zhon)
Acetic acid	(ah-seh-tik a-sid)
Adhesion	(ad-hee-zhon)
Alcohol	(al-coh-hol)
Alkaline	(al-ca-line)
Alopecia areata	(al-oh-pee-sha a-ree-ah-ta)
Alpha keratin	(al-fa keh-ra-tin)
Amino acid	(am-ee-noh a-sid)
Ammonia	(am-oh-nee-a)
Androgenic alopecia	(an-droh-jen-ik al-oh-pee-sha)
Asymmetric	(ay-sim-et-rik)
Barbicide	(bar-bee-side)
Canities	(can-it-eez)
Capillary	(cap-ill-ah-ree)
Catagen	(cat-a-jen)
Ceramic	(sir-am-ic)
Cetrimide	(set-rim-ide)
Cicatricial alopecia	(sik-at-rik-al al-oh-pee-sha)
Collodion	(coll-odd-ee-on)
Contraindication	(con-tra-in-dik-ay-shon)
Cysteine	(siss-teen)
Defamatory	(de-fam-a-tor-ee)
Dermal papilla	(der-mal pa-pil-a)
Dermatitis	(der-ma-ty-tiss)
Diffuse alopecia	(dy-fuze al-oh-pee-sha)
Di-sulphide	(dy-sull-fyd)
Effleurage	(eff-loor-arj)
Epidermis	(ep-ee-der-miss)
Eumelanin	(you-mel-ah-nin)
Follicle	(fol-ik-al)
Folliculitis	(fol-ik-you-ly-tiss)
Fragilitas crinium	(fraj-ill-it-ass krin-ee-um)
Hexachlorophene	(hex-a-klor-oh-feen)
Hydrogen	(hy-droh-jen)
Hydrophilic	(hy-droh-fill-ik)

Hydrophobic	(hy-droh-foe-bik)
Hygroscopic	(hy-groh-skop-ik)
Keloid	(kel-oyd)
Keratin	(ke-ra-tin)
Lanolin	(lan-oh-lin)
Lanugo	(lan-oo-goh)
Libellous	(ly-bell-uss)
Magnesium	(mag-nee-zee-um)
Medulla	(meh-yuh-la)
Melanin	(mel-a-nin)
Melanocytes	(mel-a-no-syts)
Monilethrix	(mon-ill-ee-thriks)
Oxymelanin	(ox-ee-mel-a-nin)
Pediculosis capitis	(ped-ik-yew-loh-sis cap-it-iss)
Petrissage	(pet-ree-sarj)
Pheomelanin	(fee-oh-mel-a-nin)
Pityriasis capitis	(pit-ih-ry-ah-sis cap-it-iss)
Polythene	(pol-ih-theen)
Porosity	(por-oss-it-ih)
Psoriasis	(sor-eye-ah-siss)
Scabies	(scay-bees)
Sebaceous cyst	(seb-ay-shus sist)
Seborrhoea	(seb-or-ee-ah)
Sodium hydroxide	(soh-dee-um hy-drok-side)
Sulphur	(sul-fuhr)
Telogen	(tel-oh-jen)
Tinea capitis	(tin-ee-ah cap-eye-tiss)
Trichologist	(try-kol-oh-jist)
Trichorrhexis nodosa	(tri-kor-rex-iss noh-doh-sa)
Vellus	(vel-uss)
Zinc pyrithione	(zink py-rith-ee-on)

1

Introduction

This chapter explains how to use this book. It is also a general introduction to the hairdressing industry.

In this chapter you will learn about:

- how to use this book to help you learn more and have fun in the process

- development routes and career prospects

- how to gain information that will help you in the industry.

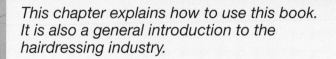

Why do you want to be a hairdresser?

Well, I am sure we all have different answers to this question but I bet most are similar. My answer would have been something like: 'Because it is an amazing industry to work in. It is wide-ranging as well as being creative and you get to meet lots of really nice people.'

Hairdressing is so much more than cutting hair with scissors! Each chapter of this book therefore covers an important area such as colouring, perming, styling and more.

In this first chapter we look at the information you will need to know if you wish to work as a hairdresser or barber, including career prospects, opportunity for development and gaining helpful information.

1.1 How to use this book

Introduction

Most of all, relax, take your time, and enjoy it!

This book is fine if used just on its own. However, if used in conjunction with the associated online learning material, it is even better. Most of the text and images are the same on screen and in this book – the resources on screen may be larger and animations and videos are often used. Lots of learning activities are included, either in boxes to the side, or at the end of each chapter. These are a great way to learn so complete them as you work through the book.

You may be accessing the computer based materials through a college or training centre. However, the learning screens, questions, activities (and more!) are also available if you are at home from: www.atthairdressing.com

Website WWW

www.atthairdressing.com

You will also find a forum where you can talk to other students and teachers as well as links to other useful sites and resources.

Structure

This textbook is set out in chapters that cover the mandatory and optional units needed for a qualification. Each chapter is split into sections and has activity sheets at the end. Remember, the structure of the computer based material is exactly the same. At the start of each chapter you will find a page showing the contents with the free online multimedia materials colour coded as follows:

Hairdressing: Level 3, ATT Training, 978-0-415-52868-9

Website
www.atthairdressing.com

CHAPTER 2 HEALTH AND SAFETY: CONTENTS, SCREENS AND ACTIVITIES

Key:
Sections from the book are set in this colour
Screens available online are set in this colour
Online activity screens are set in this colour

Photographs and diagrams

Some of the photographs and diagrams in this book may need information to be added (labels, sketches, notes, etc.). Use the online or computer based material to find out what should be added to the book. In some cases there may be a blank space where a diagram or information from the computer screen should be drawn or written.

Use this book as a workbook, make notes, underline things, make sketches and highlight important points. However, you should only do this if you own it; if it is a library or college book, use a separate piece of paper!

Margin boxes

Throughout the book you will find lots of boxes in the margins similar to those shown here:

Safety first
Important health and safety points will be highlighted here.

Key information
Special and important facts that you should remember will be added in boxes like this.

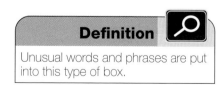

Definition
Unusual words and phrases are put into this type of box.

Website
www.atthairdressing.com

Website WWW

www.atthairdressing.com

Glossary

There is a comprehensive glossary at the back of this book. It is also available online at www.atthairdressing.com where you can search for important words and phrases and even translate them into other languages.

Useful words

We have also added a guide to the pronunciation of unusual words in this format: (proh-nun-see-ay-shun), at the front of the book. This method is called phonetic spelling, and is not perfect but will help!

Activities

Online activities are a very important part of the book and you should use them as you work through the text. When you see the following symbol, carry out the activity stated by going to the website and completing the interactive multimedia screen.

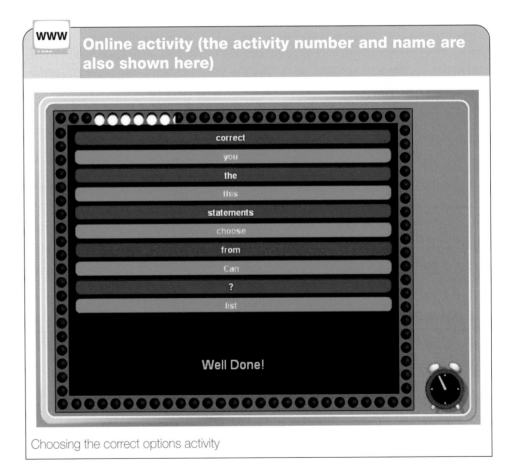

WWW **Online activity (the activity number and name are also shown here)**

correct

you

the

this

statements

choose

from

Can

?

list

Well Done!

Choosing the correct options activity

WORKSHEETS

Worksheets

As well as the 'Activity' boxes there are some worksheets available online, an example of which is presented at the end of each main chapter. You can carry out these tasks during your study of a chapter or unit, or at the end. If your college or company is registered with ATT Training, lots more of these activity sheets are available. Please visit **www.atthairdressing.com** for more details.

Assessment

There are multiple-choice quizzes available online and you should do these after you have studied a complete unit. You will see the following icon at the end of each chapter:

Website
www.atthairdressing.com

Online multiple-choice quiz **?**

. . . and good luck in the final exam, which will be arranged by your tutor/assessor.

Online multiple-choice quiz

You can also print a certificate of achievement – but only if you answer all the questions correctly of course!

1.2 Development routes and career prospects

You can train to become a hairdresser or barber in the following ways:

- Colleges and training providers offer full- or part-time NVQ (National Vocational Qualification), SVQ (Scottish Vocational Qualification) and VRQ (Vocationally Related Qualification) courses in awards, certificates or diplomas.
- Trainees are taken on at salons which allow you to learn from colleagues, take part in training in-house and attend a day-release programme at college.
- If you are still at school then there are courses that you can become involved in which will lead you on to the above steps.

There are four different levels of work in hairdressing and therefore the training courses and qualifications are set to match these levels. This book covers the knowledge required for Level 3.

Table 1.1 Levels of work

Level 1	Level 2	Level 3	Level 4:
This is often the place where school leavers start and can include work such as shampooing, conditioning and helping with work such as perming and colouring as well as supporting the rest of the team and helping clients.	This can be thought of as the junior stylist or barber and will include cutting, colouring and more complex tasks.	A stylist or senior stylist will be at this level and above. It will include more complex work such as consultations as well as supervision of others.	At this level you will usually be employed in management of a large salon or arranging shows and exhibitions.

Once you are trained as a stylist you can then take short courses in specialist areas, e.g. colouring, hair extensions, etc. through manufacturers, hair shows and seminars. Some colleges and universities offer higher level qualifications once you are experienced in hairdressing. For more information you can visit the government website www.direct.gov.uk.

The salons in which we may work are many and varied, but there are also lots of other places where a good hairdresser can work. Here are some examples but I am sure there are more:

- leisure clubs and gyms
- health and fitness clubs
- spa industry
- fashion/photographic industry
- film/television/theatre
- clients' homes
- cruise liners
- clinics and hospitals
- residential homes
- holiday resorts and hotels
- department stores
- product manufacturer and suppliers.

The type of career path we take can also be varied. Vidal Sassoon, Nicky Clarke and Lee Stafford all started at the bottom and worked their way to the top. We won't all do that but just being a good stylist in a salon is a great job, or you may end up running your own salon or working in television or films.

Here are some examples of more varied roles in our industry that may interest you:

- Trichologist:
  Clients with scalp or hair disorders may need to be referred to a doctor, but in many cases a trichologist, who is a specialist in hair and scalp disorders, may be the best choice. It takes a few years to qualify but it can be a fascinating career.
- Management:
  Many hairdressers go on to run their own salon, which means you will need management skills. You could also take on a managerial role in a large salon or even manage training courses for new students.
- TV, film and theatre:
  The creative industries are difficult to get into as there are not many openings. However, never let that put you off; if you are determined you will get there in the end with enthusiasm and hard work.
- Manufacturers:
  The large manufacturers need sales representatives, technical representatives and demonstrators for their products.
- Teaching:
  A career in teaching a skill such as hairdressing usually follows significant experience in the industry and will also require additional qualifications.
- Writing books and learning materials:
  And of course you may have ambitions to write a book – we did and here it is!

Whatever career path you follow in hairdressing it will be interesting, challenging and exciting, so go on out there and have fun!

1.3 Helpful information

This section explains the services that are offered, job roles available and how you can become a hairdresser/barber. If more information is needed some organisations that can help are highlighted throughout this section.

Gaining information about the hairdressing industry

If you are interested in training to become a hairdresser, you can find information from:

- the Internet
- magazines/trade journals
- course leaflets/prospectuses
- education and training providers
- awarding bodies such as City & Guilds, VTCT, Edexcel
- job centres
- organisations specialising in professional career guidance
- shows/seminars
- advertisements/word of mouth
- work experience
- Habia (sector skills council).

Figure 1.1 Shows can be a useful source of information

Hairdressing salons do not just offer haircutting services. They offer a great range of services. The different types of salon will specialise in their own types of services. They do not often specialise in all of the services, as it is based on their clients' wishes.

Occupational roles within the hair industry

You should understand all the job titles and roles in the salon. These include:

- shampooist
- junior/trainee
- receptionist
- junior stylist/stylist
- colour technician
- artistic director
- manager
- salon owner
- barber.

Key information

Hairdressing services may include:

- shampooing and conditioning
- cutting and blow-drying
- styling and dressing
- colouring
- perming
- relaxing
- shaving
- facial haircutting
- face massage
- scalp massage
- Indian head massage.

Figure 1.2 Dispensing shampoo

Shampooist

The shampooist, who, as the name suggests, shampoos the clients' hair and prepares them for the stylist. They may also look after the wash basin area.

Figure 1.3 A junior/trainee will assist by shampooing clients' hair

Junior/trainee

The junior or trainee works under the direction of a higher ranking member of staff. They help with many different tasks including assisting with clients (getting refreshments, taking coats, etc.), shampooing, perming, colouring, styling, blow-drying and reception duties.

Figure 1.4 The receptionist will take bookings

Receptionist

The receptionist attends to visitors and enquiries, answers the telephone, takes bookings for appointments, takes and records payments for services and retail items. He/she will also maintain the reception area.

Figure 1.5 The stylist provides hair care services to enhance appearance

Junior stylist/stylist

The junior stylist will carry out only basic hairdressing services on the client, guided by a stylist. The stylist provides hair care services to enhance the client's appearance. They deliver a wide range of services including giving advice, styling, cutting and colouring.

Colour (chemical) technician

The colour technician specialises in the application of tint to clients' hair. Therefore they have an in-depth knowledge of the use of chemicals in salons. Many will also offer other chemical services, for example perming and relaxing.

Figure 1.6 The colour technician specialises in the application of colour

Artistic director

Artistic directors are responsible for all hairdressing design work. This will include any publicity and promotional work for the salon. They also help with management of the salon and training of staff.

Figure 1.7 Artistic directors are responsible for design work

Manager

The manager participates in the smooth running of the salon on a day to day basis. He/she normally is responsible for:

- overseeing the team in the salon
- employing staff
- organising training and promotions
- ordering supplies
- paying bills.

It is up to the salon manager to ensure the salon is a profitable business whilst adhering to health and safety legislation.

Figure 1.8 The manager ensures that the salon runs smoothly

Salon owner

The salon owner may also be the manager of the salon and he/she usually carries out a wide range of business tasks. Many salon owners will also style clients' hair.

Tasks that the owner may carry out include:

- hiring employees
- dealing with customer queries/complaints
- overseeing health and safety policy and legal requirements
- ordering stock and supplies
- pricing retail products
- creating new business
- managing finances.

Figure 1.9 The salon owner may order stock and supplies

Figure 1.10 Barbers specialise in men's hair

Barber

Barbers specialise in the styling of men's hair. This includes cutting hair and maintaining facial hair or shaving.

Employment characteristics

There are many different options when working in the hair industry. Your employment characteristics could be as follows:

- full- or part-time
- self-employed
- employed seasonally.

Some staff are employed on certain days of the week only, for example on a Saturday. This may be the case early on in your career. Your hours of work can vary from day to day. Many salons have 'late night openings' on certain days and you may be required to work until closing. Renting a chair is another choice that you may be given at some point through your hairdressing career. This allows you to be self-employed and you would pay the salon to use their space and facilities.

Figure 1.11 You may rent a chair within a salon

Career patterns

Your first role when you start working in the hairdressing industry will usually be as a trainee. From here you can progress to becoming a stylist, then a senior stylist. Once you have reached this stage you can move into management if you wish. The speed of your progression will not only depend on the training and qualifications you achieve but also how well you work within the salon. Most salons have their own career progression paths that you will follow once you start working.

Figure 1.12 You will usually start work as a trainee

Key information

The speed of your progression will not only depend on the training and qualifications you achieve but also how well you work within the salon.

Organisation types

As a hairdresser you may need to access the following organisations:

- salons
- professional membership organisations
- industry lead bodies
- manufacturers and suppliers.

Salons

Salons offer hairdressing services and products to meet clients' requirements. A great deal of experience can be gained working in a salon whilst training to become a hairdresser or barber.

Figure 1.13 A salon (Kennadys in Ingatestone, Essex)

Professional membership organisations

One of the roles of this type of organisation is to allow hairdressers or barbers to be state registered. Becoming an SRH (state registered hairdresser) gives you official recognition under the Hairdressers Registration Act. The Hairdressing Council is an example of this type of organisation. Professional membership organisations will also provide information about ethical issues and legislation within the industry.

Industry lead bodies

The lead body organisations' (or sector skills councils') main role is to set the standards for a particular industry, e.g. hair and beauty. Qualifications are formed from these standards. These bodies are appointed by the government.

Figure 1.14 Lead bodies set standards which form qualifications

Manufacturers and suppliers

These organisations make and supply products and other equipment, e.g. brushes, hair dryers, rollers etc. that salons both use and sell on to the client. You may come into contact with manufacturers and suppliers if you have to return items, check their pricing or find out the ingredients of products.

Figure 1.15 Manufacturers make the products used in the salon.

1.4 Preparing for assessments

1.4.1 Simple steps

Assessment can be a stressful time for a student. However, there are some simple steps you can take to increase your confidence and performance:

1. Study the course materials as you are going along – don't leave it all to the last minute!

2. Nearer to the exam/assessment, set aside a certain time each day to practise and study.
3. Take advantage of all pre-test material in this book, online and of course any that your teacher provides.
4. Attend all revision sessions even if you feel you don't really need it.
5. Ask your teacher to clear up any uncertainties.
6. Take time off work a few days before your assessment to allow extra time to study.
7. Sleep well the night before the assessment/exam.
8. Eat a healthy breakfast the morning of your assessment to help you wake up and get your brain working.
9. Don't put too much pressure on yourself to perform.
10. Don't 'cram' too much at the last minute (for you will almost certainly forget things if you do).
11. Remember, if you worked hard to get this far you can only do your best.

1.4.2 Multiple-choice tests

Multiple-choice exams are easy for some and hard for others. The best thing about a multiple-choice quiz is that all the information you will need is given to you. The downside is that the additional information given to you is designed to make sure you really know the correct answer – and don't just guess. Here are some tips on how to prepare for a multiple-choice test:

- Practise, practise, practise.
- Do the online quizzes and other examples of the tests several times to get used to the format.
- Read all the answer options; it is often possible to rule out one or two easily so that then even if you need to guess, you have a 50:50 chance of getting it right!
- Answer ALL the questions – don't miss any out.

Figure 1.16 On reflection, you will do fine in your exams . . .

1.4.3 Practical exams

Practical work is clearly the most important part of being a hairdresser. For this reason you will have to do a number of practical examinations or tests either in your college or at your salon. These are often described as observed assessments.

If you only read one part of this section make sure it is this bit:

For your practical assessments you should:

- show a professional attitude
- look the part – be smart, clean and looking good
- not have doubts about your abilities; it will show – so be confident
- not allow other students to influence you – concentrate on your work not on that of others
- pause, relax and take a moment if you forget a procedure or process – it will come back to you
- relax and don't panic!

Remember, the job of your assessor or examiner is to make a professional judgement that you have met the necessary standards and are therefore competent to do your job. They do not want to fail you but of course they will ensure you have reached the necessary standard before saying you have passed. It is easy to feel intimidated because the assessor will not talk much and will be making notes. This is not designed to put you off; it is to make sure they are fair to everyone and that they judge you against set criteria.

They may ask you some oral questions during or after the assessment procedure. Don't panic, take your time and answer clearly and confidently.

- If you have practised and studied hard during your training, the assessments will be easy – I promise!

Personal appearance

Figure 1.17 Look good, feel good

Now, there is an old saying that I am sure you agree with: *'If you look good you feel good'.* In addition, your appearance should show the 'client' (model and an assessor in this case) that you are capable of caring for your own appearance and therefore are capable of caring for others.

Here are some important tips; you may like to add notes after each one such as how you will prepare yourself and what you will wear:

Shoes – your footwear should be comfortable, clean, polished if appropriate and in good repair (so no trainers and flip-flops then!)

Clothes – these should be professional in appearance, clean, ironed and comfortable (so no jeans and jogging suits then!)

Hair – it is very important that your own hair looks good and it should be clean and styled. Showing your assessor/examiner/client that you look after your own appearance is important (so no bed-heads then!)

Facial hair – men should ensure that they are either clean shaved or that their beard or moustache is neatly shaped and trimmed (so no one-day stubble then!)

Make-up – most people can improve their looks with a little make-up. But don't overdo it; make sure it is practical and appropriate for a day's work.

Fresh breath – if necessary use breath mints, but don't chew gum; it is very unprofessional (so you may need to get that appointment at the dentist too!)

Perfume or cologne or aftershave – in a salon, either at your work or at college, there will be many other people and odours from different products. Some clients may be allergic or sensitive to strong scents (so, the floral perfume from gran is probably not the best choice then!).

Nails – you should avoid extreme nails as they can be distracting. They should be practical so that you can carry out the procedures required for your assessments. Nails should be clean and cared for (so don't bite them during the exams!)

Personal hygiene – no client, model or examiner wants to be close to a hairdresser with bad body odour. Bath or shower daily, use deodorant and change clothes regularly (so don't jog 5 miles on your way to the exam then!)

Jewellery – keep this to a minimum – too many rings and bracelets will prevent you working properly. Excessive body jewellery such as facial piercings should not be worn as they are distracting and can look unprofessional (but don't refuse that diamond engagement ring!)

Mobile phones – these should always be turned off when working and in fact for an exam they may be prohibited (so not on vibrate, turn it off!)

2

Monitor procedures to safely control work operations

This chapter covers the NVQ/SVQ unit G22, Monitor procedures to safely control work operations; and VRQ unit 302, Carry out and monitor health and safety in the salon.

Health and safety is the responsibility of all persons at work. Senior staff, employers and supervisors in particular have a greater responsibility for health and safety than trainees.

At Level 2 stage you were responsible for your own actions in relation to health and safety. Now at Level 3 stage, you are required to monitor health and safety on a daily basis for everyone that is inside the salon. This means that it is your responsibility to ensure that everyone in the workplace is following the correct health and safety procedures.

In this chapter you will learn about:

■ checking that health and safety instructions are followed

■ making sure that risks are controlled safely and effectively.

CHAPTER 2 MONITOR PROCEDURES TO SAFELY CONTROL WORK OPERATIONS: CONTENTS, SCREENS AND ACTIVITIES

Key:

Sections from the book are set in this colour
Screens available online are set in this colour
Online activity screens are set in this colour

Check that health and safety procedures are followed

Introduction

Round the board

The Health and Safety at Work Act etc. 1974 1

The Health and Safety at Work Act etc. 1974 2

The Management Regulations

Correct selection

Risk assessments

Assigning proficient people

Communicating information

Training

Round the board

Maintaining records

Other regulations

Control of Substances Hazardous to Health 1

Control of Substances Hazardous to Health 2

Personal Protective Equipment at Work Regulations 1992 (PPE)

Electricity at Work Regulations 1989

The Workplace (Health, Safety and Welfare) Regulations 1992

The Provision and Use of Work Equipment Regulations 1998

Health and Safety (First Aid) Regulations

Manual Handling Operations Regulations 1992

Reporting of Injuries, Diseases and Dangerous Occurrences Regulations Act 1995 (RIDDOR)

Fire Precautions (Workplace) Regulations 1971

Health and Safety (Display Screen Equipment) Regulations 1992

Environmental Protection Act 1990

Five in a row

Make sure that risks are controlled safely and effectively

Introduction

Risk assessment

Likely hazards

Wordsearch

Identify who might be hurt and how

Risks associated with the hazards and avoiding these risks

Identify the risks

Avoiding risks

Record findings, implementation and reviewing

Five in a row

Methods of sterilisation

Lifting and handling objects

Dermatitis

Personal presentation and hygiene

Worksheet – Identify who might be hurt and how

Online multiple choice quiz

2.1 Check that health and safety procedures are followed

When monitoring health and safety in the salon, you must be up to date with all regulations and workplace instructions.

Figure 2.1 You will be required to take an active role in helping your employer

Online activity 2.1 WWW

Round the board

The Health and Safety at Work Act etc.1974

This Act places a strict duty on employers to ensure, so far as is reasonably practicable, safe working conditions and the absence of risks to health in connection with the use, handling, storage and transport of articles and substances.

Under the Health and Safety at Work Act an employer must provide:

- safe equipment and safe systems of work
- safe handling, storage and transport of substances
- a safe place of work with safe access and exit
- a safe working environment with adequate welfare facilities
- all necessary information, instruction, training and supervision
- all necessary personal protective equipment free of charge.

Figure 2.2 Employers must provide a safe environment

The Management Regulations

These regulations give details on how employers can follow the Health and Safety at Work etc. Act. It outlines what they must do in relation to all work activities. These duties include:

- carrying out risk assessments and arranging measures identified
- assigning proficient staff to help put the measures into practice
- giving clear information to employees
- providing training to employees.

Online activity 2.2

Correct selection

Risk assessments

Definition

Risk assessment: The process of calculating the risk associated with a hazard and the actions taken to avoid it.

Risk assessments must be carried out by employers or their competent appointed staff (who could be you). They should be carried out at regular intervals which will be established by workplace instructions. The procedure of carrying out a risk assessment will be covered in the next section, 'Make sure that risks are controlled safely and effectively'.

Figure 2.3 Risk assessment will be carried out by taking a look around the salon

Assigning proficient people

Employers will usually put staff in charge of carrying out risk assessments. This may be part of your job role. All staff must be fully competent in these health and safety duties, including promptly taking action to remove or reduce any risks there may be.

Figure 2.4 Your employer may put you in charge of risk assessments

Safety first

All staff must be fully competent in these health and safety duties, including promptly taking action to remove or reduce any risks there may be.

Figure 2.5 Displaying health and safety rules and regulations

Communicating information

As a senior member of staff it will be your role to ensure that health and safety is communicated clearly to everyone that is in the salon. Every salon must by law display its health and safety rules and regulations on the wall in a position that can be seen by everyone. Other written communication can be used to inform staff of any aspects of health and safety, for example leaflets.

In addition verbal communication can be used to give out information, for example through team meetings, to inform staff of any changes or new courses to attend. You may also tell other staff of any potential hazards that you may spot around the salon. Ensure that you gain feedback from others in the salon, as this will ensure that the information you are providing is clear and easily understood.

Figure 2.6 Team meetings allow you to inform staff of health and safety procedures

Training

You should identify if staff (this includes yourself) need any training on health and safety issues. When this has been established, it must be reported to management, so that appropriate action can be taken.

Safety first ⚠️

Ensure that training is provided for everyone who needs it.

Figure 2.7 Identify whether staff need any training

Online activity 2.3 www

Round the board

Maintaining records

All health and safety records must be maintained including details of the following:

- risk assessments
- accidents that have occurred in the salon, i.e. using the accident book
- tests that have been carried out, i.e. electrical equipment checks.

All records must conform to both legal and your own salon's requirements. Only those people who are authorised to, can access these records.

Figure 2.8 Records must only be accessed by those authorised

Other regulations

Ensure that you have up-to-date knowledge on the following regulations.

- Control of Substances Hazardous to Health Regulations (COSHH)
- Personal Protective Equipment at Work Regulations (PPE)
- Electricity at Work Regulations
- Workplace (Health, Safety and Welfare) Regulations
- Provision and Use of Work Equipment Regulations
- Health and Safety (First Aid) Regulations
- Manual Handling Operations Regulations
- Reporting of Injuries, Diseases and Dangerous Occurrences Regulations (RIDDOR)
- Fire Precautions (Workplace) Regulations
- Health and Safety (Display Screen Equipment) Regulations
- Environmental Protection Act.

There are also local bye-laws which are specific to the area where the salon is situated. Both you and your employer must adhere to these regulations.

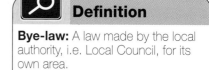

Definition

Bye-law: A law made by the local authority, i.e. Local Council, for its own area.

Figure 2.9 Hazardous substance symbols showing that materials are flammable, corrosive, harmful/irritant and (very) toxic

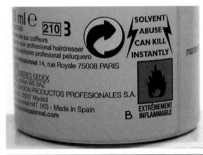

Figure 2.10 Hazard symbol shown on a product

Control of Substances Hazardous to Health Regulations 2002

These are commonly called the COSHH regulations and they lay down the essential requirements for controlling exposure to hazardous substances and for protecting people who may be affected by them.

A substance is considered to be hazardous if it can cause harm to the body. It only poses a risk if it is:

- inhaled (breathed in)
- ingested (swallowed)
- in contact with the skin
- absorbed through the skin
- injected into the body
- introduced into the body via cuts etc.

Personal Protective Equipment at Work Regulations 1992 (PPE)

The requirements under this Act will be met when you comply with the COSHH regulations. These regulations require every employer to provide suitable personal protective equipment (PPE) to each of his or her employees who may be exposed to any risk while at work.

The PPE supplied must be properly maintained and the users must be trained and monitored to ensure that the PPE is properly used. Employees are required to report to the employer any loss of or damage to PPE.

In the average salon, PPE will include the use of gloves and wearing tinting aprons when handling perm lotion, relaxers, tints and bleach, and possibly eye protection when handling and mixing strong bleach solutions. It is the duty of the workforce to use PPE when required.

Key information

Under the COSHH regulations employers must:

- identify substances in the workplace which are potentially hazardous
- assess the risk to health from exposure to the hazardous substances and record the results
- make an assessment as to which members of staff are at risk
- look for alternative, less hazardous substances and substitute if possible
- decide what precautions are required
- introduce effective measures to prevent or control the exposure
- inform, instruct and train all members of staff
- review the assessment on a regular basis.

Activity

The associated learning screen for this part is interactive.

Figure 2.11 Gloves and aprons should be worn

Electricity at Work Regulations 1989

These regulations state that you must:

- Always check electrical equipment before using it. Look for loose wires and check that the plug is not cracked or damaged in any way. Check that the cord is not frayed or cracked.
- Never use electrical equipment when your hands are wet.
- Electrical equipment should be maintained regularly and checked by a suitably qualified person. Once checked the equipment should have a certificate or label acknowledging it.
- Faulty electrical equipment in the workplace must be removed, labelled as faulty and reported to the relevant person.

⚠ Safety first

Employees are required to report to the employer any loss of or damage to PPE.

Figure 2.12 Checking electrical equipment for damage

Figure 2.13 Correct labelling of faulty equipment

The Workplace (Health, Safety and Welfare) Regulations 1992

This Act states that the employer is to provide a safe working environment for employees and members of the public. The employer must legally:

- maintain equipment
- regulate temperature
- ensure adequate lighting.

It is the responsibility of the employee to work safely to ensure the safety of clients and colleagues.

Figure 2.14 Employers must provide a safe working environment

The Provision and Use of Work Equipment Regulations 1998

The following requirements apply to all equipment:

- Work equipment must be suitable for the purpose for which it is used.
- Equipment must be properly maintained and a maintenance log kept, for example for portable electrical hand tools.
- Users and supervisors of equipment must be given adequate health and safety training and written instructions where required.

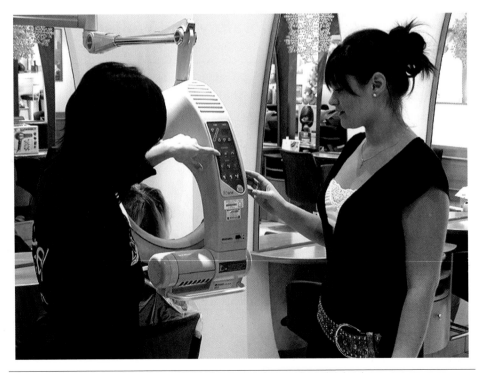

Figure 2.15 Equipment must be suitable for use and properly maintained

Health and Safety (First Aid) Regulations

These regulations state that employers must ensure that equipment and facilities that are adequate and appropriate for administering first aid to employees are available. All establishments should have a registered first-aider and a stocked first aid box.

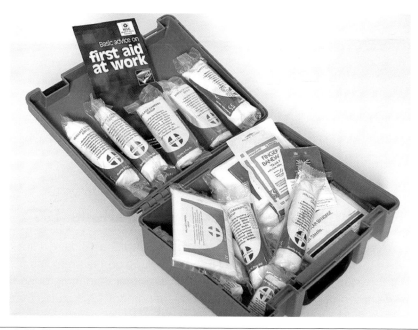

Figure 2.16 First aid kit

Manual Handling Operations Regulations 1992

These regulations cover the lifting of loads as well as lowering, pushing, pulling, carrying and moving them, whether by hand or other bodily force. You should carry out an assessment of the risks involved by looking at the following:

- the weight of the load
- the shape of the load (e.g. some loads may not be particularly heavy but can be awkward to lift)
- the working environment (e.g. if the area is damp the employee's hands could be wet and the load might slip)
- where the task is to be carried out (e.g. are there cramped conditions which make it difficult to lift)
- the individual's capability.

Key information

The Manual Handling Operations Regulations cover the lifting of loads as well as lowering, pushing, pulling, carrying and moving them, whether by hand or other bodily force.

Reporting of Injuries, Diseases and Dangerous Occurrences Regulations Act 1995 (RIDDOR)

The Act states that work related accidents, diseases and dangerous occurrences must be reported. You must keep these records for three years and they can be in written form and kept in a file, or stored in a computer file. Records are to include:

- date and method of reporting
- date, time and place of event
- personal details of those involved
- brief description.

Figure 2.17 Records can be in written form . . .   **Figure 2.18** . . . or electronic

Fire Precautions (Workplace) Regulations 1971

The employer must comply with the fire regulations and should have a fire certificate if there are more than twenty people working on the premises at once or if there are more than ten working on floors other than the ground floor. The Fire Precautions (Workplace) Regulations Amendment 1999 states that the employer must be responsible for carrying out a fire risk assessment and produce an evacuation plan in an emergency. They must also inform and train employees about fire precautions. They must choose a designated person to help.

Figure 2.19 Fire extinguisher and fire blanket

Health and Safety (Display Screen Equipment) Regulations 1992

These regulations protect users of computers and other similar equipment in the workplace. High use can lead to risk of eye strain, muscular pain and even mental stress and as more and more salons are using computers, this is becoming an important consideration.

Figure 2.20 Legislation protects employees who use computers

Environmental Protection Act 1990

The correct disposal of waste is covered by these regulations. This is particularly important as hairdressers work with products that contain chemicals. All waste in the salon must be disposed of in a way that will not pollute the environment or cause harm to other people. Employers have the following responsibilities under this Act:

- to dispose of waste in a safe manner
- to provide training to employees for safe disposal of waste
- to contact manufacturers of the products to gain information on safe disposal.

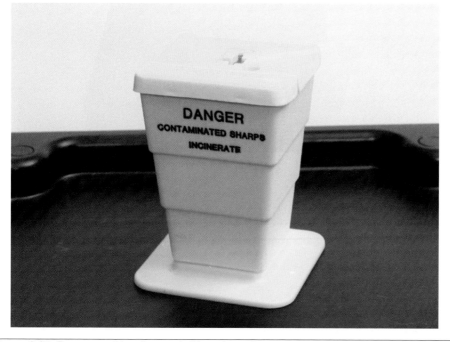

Figure 2.21 Razors must be disposed of in a sharps box

www Online activity 2.4

Five in a row

2.2 Make sure that risks are controlled safely and effectively

Risk assessments should be carried out to control risks in the workplace. This section covers the way in which they are carried out in the salon.

Risk assessment

To carry out a risk assessment you should:

- identify likely hazards
- identify who can be hurt and how
- decide risks associated with the hazards and how to avoid these risks
- record findings and implementation
- review and update assessments if necessary.

Figure 2.22 Carrying out risk assessment

Likely hazards

Many things around the salon can be a hazard. A hazard is a source of danger.

Examples of hazards include the following:

- electrical equipment
- storage boxes
- products
- trailing leads.

Key information

A hazard is a source of danger.

Online activity 2.5 WWW

Wordsearch

Identify who might be hurt and how

When you have established the hazards, you must decide who could be harmed by them. List those that may be affected by the hazard in groups, for example, 'staff' may be affected by 'lifting heavy boxes into storeroom' whereas 'everyone' will be affected by a 'loose floor tile'. You must also decide how the group may be injured, for example 'regularly lifting heavy boxes may cause a back injury'.

Figure 2.23 Staff may be affected by lifting heavy boxes

Risks associated with the hazards and avoiding these risks

A risk is the likelihood of an accident occurring from the hazard. Each of the previously mentioned hazards is covered here, along with the actions to be taken to avoid them from happening (risk assessment).

Figure 2.24 Electrical equipment

A risk from electrical equipment is that it may cause somebody an injury when using or repairing it. To avoid this happening it is important that staff are trained in its use and it is tested for correct working order.

Figure 2.25 Storage boxes

Storage boxes are a risk if they are stored in front of a fire exit for example. There is a strong likelihood that they will cause an accident. The boxes must be moved to an area that does not cause a risk to staff or clients.

Figure 2.26 Products

Products can be a risk due to them containing chemicals that are flammable and toxic. They must be stored securely and only be available to hairdressers who have been trained in their use.

Figure 2.27 Trailing leads

Trailing leads are a risk if it is likely that somebody may trip over them. Make sure they are not in the passageway of a client or another member of staff.

Online activity 2.6   WWW

Identify the risks

Avoiding risks

As you will be monitoring other people's actions with regard to health and safety, you must be aware of all the precautions to take in the salon. Regular meetings are an excellent method of communicating this information to everyone in the salon.

Figure 2.28 Regular meetings give the opportunity to get information across

Record findings, implementation and reviewing

Keep the recordings simple as shown in Table 2.1. The risk assessment should be carried out at regular intervals. Setting a date in the future will ensure that the review takes place. Inform your manager or salon owner if any risks are not resolved in accordance with your risk assessment.

Table 2.1 Findings of a risk assessment

Hazard	The risk	To whom	Level of risk	How the risk can be controlled	When
Water on the floor in salon	Slipping	Everyone	Low	Mopped up Put sign out to indicate 'wet floor'	Straight away
Loose tile in the salon	Tripping	Everyone	High	Must be repaired	Specify date for repair
Untidy staff room	Tripping	Staff	Medium	Inform staff All staff to tidy up after themselves	Checked each week

Ring the bell by clicking true or false. You must get five in a row correct. If you answer one incorrectly you must start again.

Colours and lighteners are chemical free.

Figure 2.29 Online activity screen

Five in a row

Methods of sterilisation

Salons may use a variety of ways to sterilise equipment (make free of micro-organisms). Remember to always wash brushes and combs before sterilising.

Autoclave (heat)

This is the recommended method of sterilisation for small metal items. The high temperature steam produced destroys all micro-organisms.

UV cabinet (ultraviolet radiation)

Clean tools can be stored in a UV cabinet once they have been sterilised.

Key information

Remember to always wash brushes and combs before sterilising.

Figure 2.30 Autoclave and UV cabinet

Chemical sterilisation

Proprietary sterilising solutions and sprays are available for sterilising equipment. To be effective the chemical solutions should be used for the correct length of time and mixed following the manufacturer's instructions. Sterilising sprays are used for wiping scissors and clippers.

Figure 2.31 Chemical sterilising solution

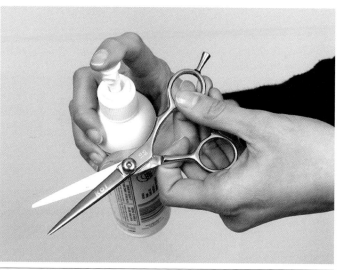

Figure 2.32 Sterilising spray

Lifting and handling objects

When lifting heavy packages keep your back straight, feet slightly apart and bend your knees. If packages are too heavy, politely ask another member of staff to help you. Always use a strong, sturdy stepladder when putting stock on a high shelf. Never use a chair to stand on. In a salon the major risk is from lifting boxes of stock items onto or off shelves.

Figure 2.33 Keep your back straight, feet slightly apart, and bend your knees

Figure 2.34 Always use a strong, sturdy stepladder when putting stock on a high shelf

Dermatitis

This is a very common skin disease in hairdressers and is caused by hands being exposed to certain products and carrying out wet work regularly. Dermatitis can be prevented by:

- ensuring shampoo and conditioner are rinsed from your hands
- drying hands thoroughly
- moisturising regularly
- wearing disposable gloves.

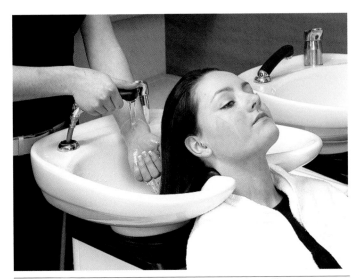

Figure 2.35 Carrying out wet work can cause dermatitis

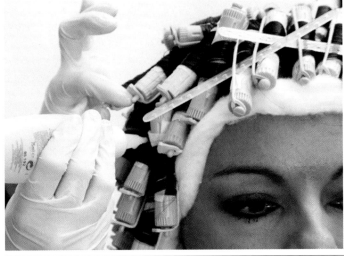

Figure 2.36 Using disposable gloves can prevent dermatitis

Personal presentation and hygiene

The stylist must always ensure his or her own personal hygiene and presentation are of a high standard. Particularly important is that hands and nails should be clean so that the risk of spreading infection is minimised. They should not be stained with hair colourant. Nails should not be bitten and should not be too long (dirt can get trapped underneath).

Figure 2.37 Ensure your own personal hygiene and presentation at all times

2.3 Worksheets

You can carry out the worksheets during your study of a chapter or unit, or at the end. An example is presented here and there are more online. If your college or company is registered with ATT Training, lots more are available. Write your answers directly in the book, but only if you own it of course – if it is a library or college book, use a separate piece of paper!

2.3.1 Identify who might be hurt and how

When you have established any potential hazards, you must decide who could be harmed by them. List those that may be affected by the hazard in groups; for example, 'staff' may be affected by 'lifting heavy boxes into storeroom' whereas 'everyone' will be affected by a 'loose floor tile'. You must also decide how the group may be injured, for example 'regularly lifting heavy boxes may cause a back injury'.

Complete this table using examples of hazards that may occur in the salon

Hazard	Who may be affected	How may they be affected
Loose floor tile	Everyone – staff, customers, visitors	Someone may trip over the tile by catching their shoe

2.4 Assessment

Well done! If you have studied all the content of this unit you may be ready to test your knowledge.

Check out the 'Preparing for assessments' section in Chapter 1 if you have not already done so, and always remember:

- You can only do your best if you have...
  - studied hard
  - completed the activities
  - completed the worksheets
  - practised, practised, practised
  - and then revised!

? Now carry out the online multiple-choice quiz

... and good luck in the final exam, which will be arranged by your tutor/assessor.

Consultations

This chapter covers the NVQ/SVQ unit G21, Provide hairdressing consultation services; and VRQ unit 303, Consultation support for colleagues on hair services.

In this chapter, you will learn about the way to carry out thorough and effective consultations starting with finding out your clients' requirements and following on to making recommendations based on individual client factors.

In this chapter you will learn about:

- identifying client needs and wishes
- analysing the hair, skin and scalp
- making recommendations to clients
- advising clients on hair maintenance and management
- agreeing services with your client.

CHAPTER 3 CONSULTATIONS: CONTENTS, SCREENS AND ACTIVITIES

Key:
Sections from the book are set in this colour
Screens available online are set in this colour
Online activity screens are set in this colour

Identify client's needs and wishes

Introduction
Communication
Verbal communication
Open and closed questioning skills
Drag into correct group

Non-verbal communication/body language
Listening
Level 3 consultation
Round the board

Analyse the hair, skin and scalp

Introduction
Skin structure
Layers of a strand of hair
Hair growth cycle
Wordsearch
Hair texture and density
Hair and skin testing
Porosity test
Elasticity test
Incompatibility test
Skin test
Pre-perm test curl
Test cutting
Development test curl
Strand/colour test
Shoot the target
Hair and scalp conditions
Non-contagious – damaged cuticle
Pityriasis capitis (dandruff)
Seborrhoea
Fragilitas crinium (split ends)
Trichorrhexis nodosa
Monilethrix
Acne
Eczema
Psoriasis

Check it
Ingrowing hair
Alopecia (baldness)
Androgenic alopecia (male pattern baldness)
Diffuse alopecia
Alopecia areata
Traction alopecia
Cicatricial alopecia
Check it
Sebaceous cyst
Warts
Canities (grey hair)
Contagious – folliculitis
Tinea capitis (ringworm of the scalp)
Impetigo
Pediculosis capitis (head lice)
Scabies
Drag Into correct group
Hair growth patterns 1
Head and face shapes 1
Head and face shapes 2
Head and face shapes 3
Head and face shapes 4
Five in a row
Helping colleagues

Make recommendations to clients

Introduction
Current fashion trends
Alternative services and products

Referrals to other salons
Referrals to a pharmacist, GP or trichologist
Five in a row

Advise clients on hair maintenance and management

Introduction
Identify the client's current hair care routine

Improving on the client's current routine
Products and heated styling equipment

Agree services with your client

Introduction
Correct selection
Record keeping

Legislation related to products and services
Worksheet – Current fashion trends
Online multiple choice quiz

3.1 Identify client's needs and wants

Communication

There are many methods of communicating with your client to gain the information you need to carry out the service.

Verbal communication

This type of communication involves speaking to each other. Always speak clearly without any long pauses as this may be uncomfortable. Ensure that your conversation is not too complicated; simplify if you need to so that the client is not confused by any hairdressing jargon. You will need to ask questions to find out exactly what it is the client would like. The client may find it easier to show you a picture of their ideas. Visual aids are very useful in conveying this information. They should be given time to think about what you have said and then reply to you. Clarify the information the client is giving you at regular times during the conversation.

Key information

You will use the following methods during the consultation:

- verbal communication
- non-verbal communication
- listening.

Definition

Jargon: Special words, expressions or phrases used by a particular profession that may be difficult for those outside of the profession to understand.

Figure 3.1 Visual aids can help you to communicate with your client more effectively

Open and closed questioning skills

Develop different questioning skills using both open and closed questions. Questions that require a yes or no reply are known as closed questions and help you to test your understanding.

Using words such as when, who, what, if, etc., will enable the client to discuss their needs and this method is known as open questioning. It allows you to enquire further to gain more in-depth information about the client's wishes.

Key information

An example of an open question is: *How do you feel about how you wear your hair now?*

An example of a closed question is: *Would you like me to use the same colour as last time?*

Figure 3.2 Finding out what the client wants involves asking both open and closed questions

WWW   **Online activity 3.1**

Drag into correct group

Non-verbal communication/body language

Body language is a very important form of communication. Our stance, gestures and facial expressions say a lot about how we feel; for example, smiling implies friendliness and frowning implies hostility. Your body language should be positive at all times.

Maintain eye contact with the client when talking and listening to show you are paying attention, and conveying friendliness and trust. Eye contact will also allow you to understand more about your client. Viewing their facial expressions will help you to see if they comprehend what you are saying and whether they are in agreement.

Figure 3.3 Incorrect body language

Figure 3.4 Correct body language

Listening

When the client is talking to you, you must listen very carefully to ensure that you are able to determine their requirements and understand any concerns they may have. Positive body language should be shown as this will encourage the client to really feel they can express their wishes to you. This includes nodding to show that you understand their comments or concerns, and/or that you agree with what they are saying.

Level 3 consultation

As you move from Level 2 to Level 3 experience, you will notice that relationships with your clients will improve. You will have a greater ability to communicate and empathise, which will enhance your bond with them. This will only happen in time so cannot be rushed.

As you spend more time with your clients, you'll gain an understanding of their wishes in greater detail, for example, whether you can present a different option to them, offering new hairstyles to suit them, etc. Your aim is to maintain high standards of client care at all times, in order to encourage contented customers so that they will always visit your salon and not look elsewhere. As you keep up with the ever changing world of hairdressing, you will gain invaluable experience that can be put into practice with each individual client.

 **Safety first**

When the client is talking to you, you must listen very carefully to ensure that you are able to determine their requirements and understand any concerns they may have.

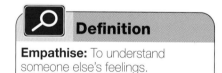 **Definition**

Empathise: To understand someone else's feelings.

Figure 3.5 You'll learn more about your clients over time

www **Online activity 3.2**

Round the board

3.2 Analyse the hair, skin and scalp

Definition

Analyse: Examine in detail, e.g. the condition of the hair, skin and scalp.

Before carrying out any kind of service on the client's hair, you must analyse the hair, skin and scalp to find out whether there are any problems that may affect the service. The condition of the hair will determine whether it is advisable to perform certain services or use particular products.

Figure 3.6 Analyse the hair, skin and scalp

Not only will you need to look at the client's hair and perform certain tests, but you will also need to ask the client questions using positive communication skills in order to find out as much information as you can about previous services. Always check the client's records. This may give you information on previous treatments and whether future services are possible.

Safety first ⚠️

In order to diagnose, the hairdresser must understand the structure of the hair and skin and the hair growth cycle.

Skin structure

The three layers of the skin are the:

- epidermis
- dermis
- subcutaneous layer.

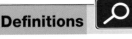
Definitions

Follicle: Sac containing the hair shaft in the epidermis.

Sebaceous gland: A gland that produces an oil secretion called sebum.

Capillary: Very thin blood vessel.

The epidermis is the top protective layer of the skin. The dermis is the central structure and contains blood vessels, nerve endings, hair follicles, sweat and sebaceous glands. The subcutaneous layer is below the dermis and it contains fatty tissues. This provides insulation and acts as a defence, protecting the organs internally. The hair follicle is attached to the dermal papilla. This is the capillary network through which the hair obtains its food and oxygen supply from the blood.

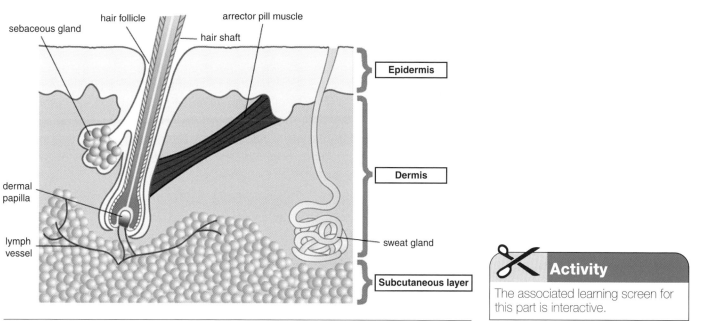

Figure 3.7 Skin structure

✂ **Activity**
The associated learning screen for this part is interactive.

Layers of a strand of hair

Diagram 3.8 shows the three layers of a strand of hair: cuticle, cortex and medulla. The cuticle is translucent (the hair colour shows through it) and has a protective function. It is made up of layers of scales. There are more layers around the base of the hair due to wear and tear at the tip. The cortex forms the bulk of the hair. In this part of the hair the chemical changes of bleaching, tinting, perming and straightening take place. Melanin and pheomelanin are found in the cortex, which gives the hair its colour. The medulla is in the centre of the hair shaft. Very fine hair does not have a medulla.

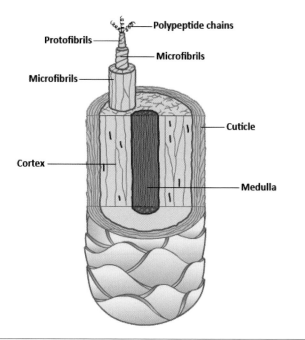

Figure 3.8 Hair structure

Hair growth cycle

Hair grows from the follicle. Hair above the skin is dead, below the skin in the follicle it is actively growing. A new hair grows for a number of years (this varies from person to person; the period is longer in young people) and then dies at the base of the follicle. The follicle rests for a few months before a new hair starts to grow. Hair grows at an average figure of 1.25 centimetres (half an inch) per month.

The terms used in this growth cycle are:

Anagen: the stage when the hair is growing from the dermal papilla. This stage may last from one to six years. Hair in different areas of the body has a shorter phase for this stage, e.g. men's facial hair.

Catagen: a time when the hair stops growing and detaches itself from the papilla and moves up the follicle. This stage lasts for about two weeks.

Telogen: the time when the follicle and papilla are in a stage of rest. There is no activity in the papilla. It lasts between three and four months.

After the telogen stage, the hair follicle will begin to grow downwards again and therefore enters the anagen phase again (early anagen). Activity within the papilla allows new hair to grow.

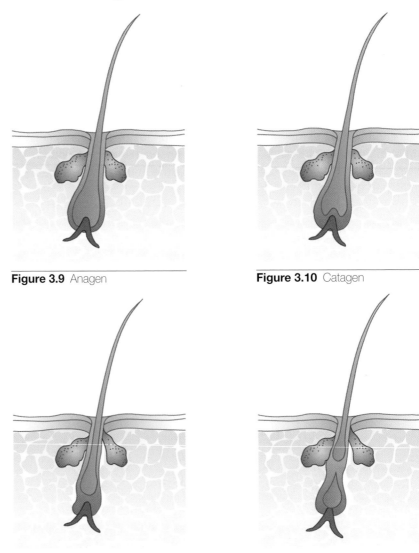

Figure 3.9 Anagen

Figure 3.10 Catagen

Figure 3.11 Telogen

Figure 3.12 Early anagen

Hair texture and density

This refers to the amount of hair that the client has on his or her head. If a client has dense hair this means that you will not be able to see the client's scalp. If you can see the client's scalp then they have a low density of hair on their head.

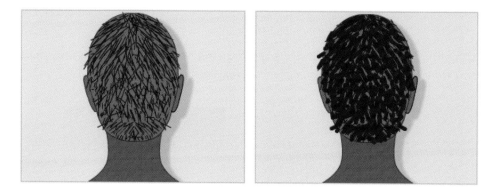

Figure 3.13 Low density of hair shown on the left, dense hair shown on the right

Hair and skin testing

To enable you to diagnose the condition of the client's hair, there are a number of tests that can be carried out. These will show you the reaction of the skin and hair to particular services.

Porosity test

The porosity test assesses the degree of damage to the cuticle. A damaged cuticle absorbs more moisture, which makes the hair feel rougher.

Method

Hold a few strands of hair at the end and slide your fingers towards the root. If it feels rough the cuticles are raised and this indicates the condition of the hair is poor. If it feels smooth the cuticles are flat and the condition of the hair is good.

Safety first

Carry out all tests by following manufacturers' instructions and your salon's policies.

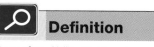

Definition

Porosity: Ability to absorb moisture.

Figure 3.14 Carrying out the porosity test

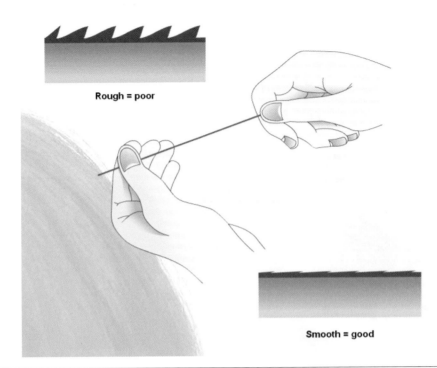

Rough = poor

Smooth = good

Figure 3.15 Raised and flat cuticles

Definition

Cortex: Middle layer of the hair shaft.

Elasticity test

This test assesses the extent of damage to the cortex of the hair. It measures the ability of the hair to be stretched.

Method
Hold a single strand of dry hair firmly at each end with finger and thumb. Pull back gently and see how much the hair stretches and springs back.

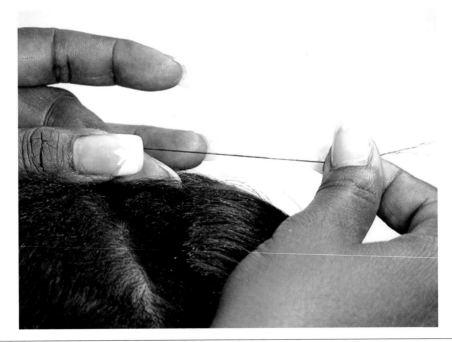

Figure 3.16 Conducting the elasticity test

A hair in good condition can stretch up to a third of its length and return to its original length. If the hair snaps it indicates that the hair has a weak cortex.

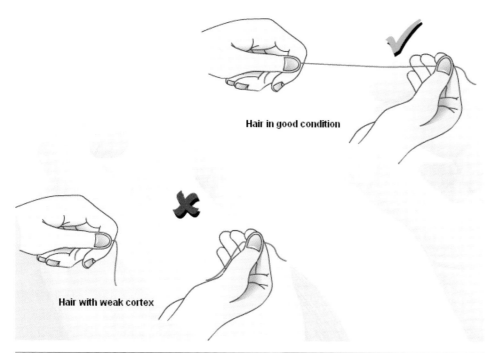

Figure 3.17 Elasticity test results

Incompatibility test

The hairdresser should make sure that any products that have been used previously on the hair do not react unfavourably with products that the hairdresser intends to use. This incompatibility test detects metallic salts used in colour preparations, so-called 'hair colour restorers', for example.

> **⚠ Safety first**
>
> The hairdresser should make sure that any products that have been used previously on the hair do not react unfavourably with products that the hairdresser intends to use.

Figure 3.18 Cut a piece of hair from the root

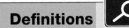

Definitions

Hydrogen peroxide: An agent used for oxidising when colouring and perming.

Ammonia: Colourless fluid used as a solvent.

Figure 3.19 Incompatibility test in progress

Safety first ⚠

About one in twenty-five clients develops a positive reaction to the test; under no circumstances should the service be completed.

Definition

Collodion: A syrupy, clean solution of pyroxylin, alcohol and ether.

Safety first ⚠

If the result of this test is unsatisfactory, do not perm.

Method

Prepare a solution of twenty parts hydrogen peroxide and one part ammonia.

Sellotape together a small group of hairs taken from the client's head, at the root end. Immerse the hairs in the solution for 30 minutes. A positive reaction will show the presence of bubbles, give off heat (the beaker gets warmer), or the hair will change colour.

Skin test

This is conducted to see if a client will develop an allergic reaction to the chemicals contained in colouring products. They are usually carried out before tinting and semi-permanent services. About one in twenty-five clients develops a positive reaction to the test; under no circumstances should the service be completed.

Method

Gown the client and prepare a solution of the chemical to be used in the salon service. Cleanse behind the ear with cotton wool and alcohol. Place a penny sized smear of the chemical on the cleansed area. To protect the area from water it may be covered with collodion. Ask the client to return after 48 hours. Redness, swelling or irritation would indicate a positive reaction and the treatment should not be supplied. Colouring companies recommend this method to comply with legal requirements.

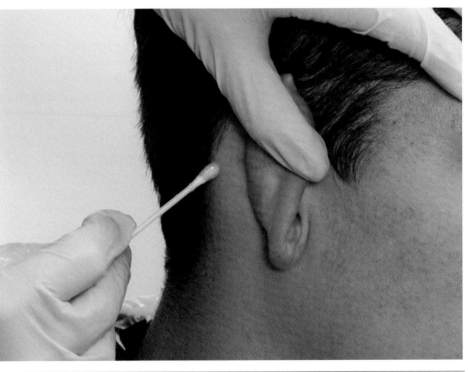

Figure 3.20 Carrying out a skin test

Pre-perm test curl

If the hair has been damaged through perming or colouring, a sample of hair should be tested to find out if the full head can be permed.

Method

Take a cutting of the hair, apply perm lotion and wind around a perm rod. Leave the hair to develop and neutralise. Dry the hair and test the elasticity strength. If the results are satisfactory, the hairdresser can continue with the perm. If the result is unsatisfactory, do not perm.

Figure 3.21 Pre-perm test curl

Test cutting

This method can be used to assess the effects of an application before the whole head is treated.

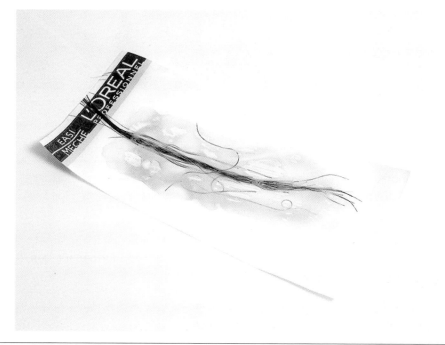

Figure 3.22 Test cutting

Method
Cut a few strands of hair and sellotape them at the roots. Immerse the strands of hair in the intended products and process according to the manufacturer's instructions. Examine the results for colour effects. Uneven colouring will indicate damaged hair and whether it can take further chemical treatment.

Development test curl

After a perm lotion has been on the hair for a certain length of time, this test can be carried out to see if the hair has reached the correct development.

Method
Unwind four rods in different sections to check development. The curl should show an 'S' shaped bend, separation of the strands, and the hair should look shiny. The curl should be checked after five minutes. Gloves must always be worn when carrying out this test.

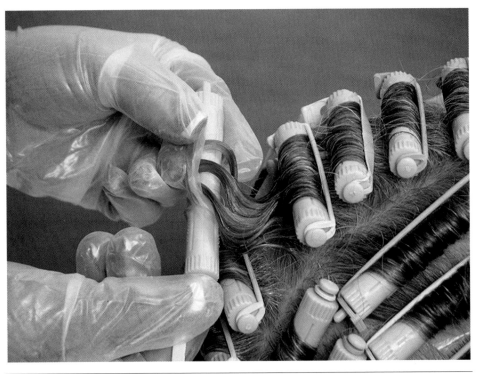

Figure 3.23 The 'S' shaped bend

Colour/strand test

This test monitors the colour development along a strand of hair during processing. This should be done before the colourant is rinsed from the hair.

Method
Remove the colourant from a small mesh of hair. Check to see if the target shade has been reached. If not, leave the colour to develop further. If it has, then remove colour.

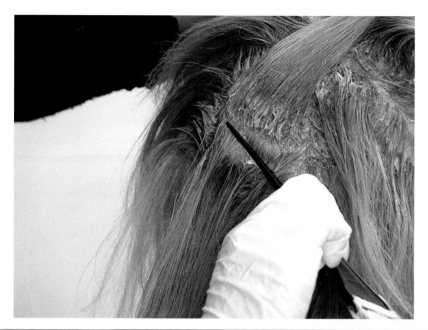

Figure 3.24 Carrying out a colour/strand test

Online activity 3.4 www

Shoot the target

Hair and scalp conditions

A hairdresser should be able to recognise abnormal hair and scalp (skin) conditions. There are two categories of abnormal conditions:

- contagious (can be caught by contact)
- non-contagious (cannot be caught by contact).

Non-contagious – damaged cuticle

The cuticle is a series of overlapping scales that form the outside layer of the hair shaft. When the cuticle is in a good condition they lie flat and feel smooth to the touch. When they are damaged they become raised and feel rough. In extreme conditions of neglect or severe chemical damage some of the cuticles break off. Physical and chemical abuse to the hair are often the causes. The application of a protein conditioner will smooth down the scales and make the hair more manageable.

> 🔍 **Definition**
>
> **Cuticle:** A series of overlapping scales that form the outer layer of the hair shaft.

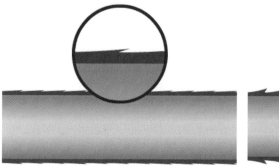

Figure 3.25 Cuticle in good condition

Figure 3.26 Cuticle in poor condition

Pityriasis capitis (dandruff)

Pityriasis capitis (dandruff) can be recognised by dry flaky scales that are shed from the scalp. Some irritation can be experienced by the client. The disorder is caused by the overproduction of skin cells. In severe cases white, grey or yellowish scales are continually falling from the scalp. This produces a breeding ground for bacteria or induces infections. Conditioners that have antiseptic properties such as cetrimide or hexachlorophene are useful for this disorder.

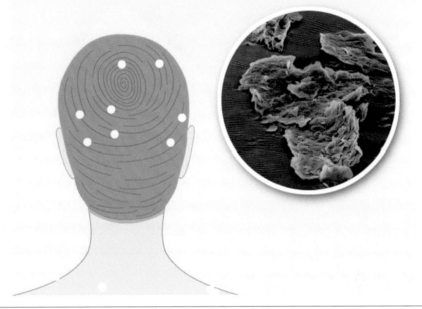

Figure 3.27 Dandruff is caused by the overproduction of skin cells

Seborrhoea

Seborrhoea is caused by the excess production of sebum from the sebaceous gland. The hair and scalp appear to be in a very oily state. Special conditioning treatments are available for this problem. Take care not to massage the scalp. If the condition is severe refer the client for medical treatment.

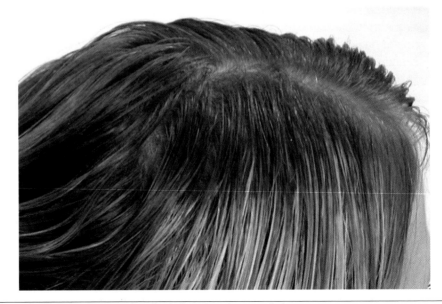

Figure 3.28 Seborrhoea makes the hair and scalp very oily in appearance

Fragilitas crinium (split ends)

Fragilitas crinium is a condition where the hair becomes very dry and brittle. Splits occur on the points of the hair shaft. It is caused by chemical and physical damage. Some conditioners enable the split ends to stick together but this is a temporary arrangement. The only real treatment is to have the hair cut.

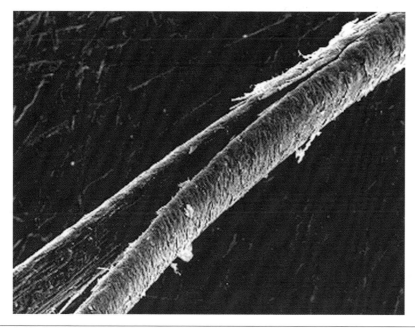

Figure 3.29 Split end

Trichorrhexis nodosa

Trichorrhexis nodosa is a condition in which areas towards the point of the hair shaft swell up. The hair fractures at this point and leaves a very broken and exposed cortex. Chemical and physical damage can cause this condition but in some cases it is due to genetic or metabolic disorders. Conditioners will improve the quality of the hair.

Key information

Chemical and physical damage can cause this condition but in some cases it is due to genetic or metabolic disorders.

Figure 3.30 Trichorrhexis nodosa

Monilethrix

This condition is caused by the uneven production of cells in the dermal papilla of the hair. The hair breaks easily, keeping the hair short or showing evidence of baldness. The cause is hereditary. No treatment is available.

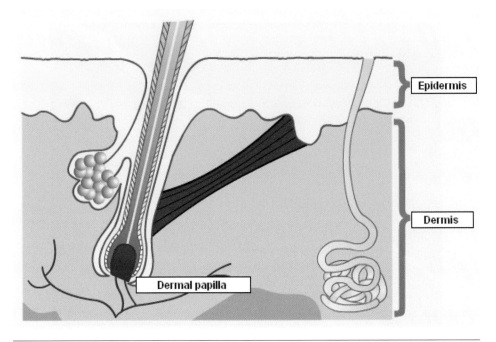

Figure 3.31 Monilethrix is caused by the uneven production of cells in the dermal papilla

Acne

Raised spots and bumps found on the skin caused by excess sebum and other matter which block the follicle. This causes a skin reaction. Normal salon services can be carried but if the condition is near the hairline, extra care must be taken. The client should be referred to their GP.

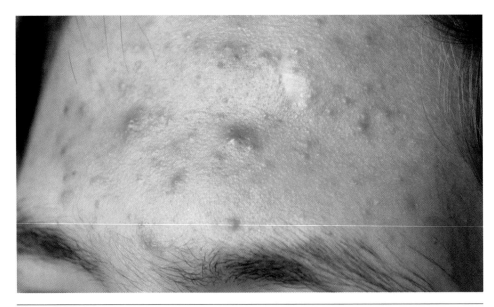

Figure 3.32 Acne

Eczema

This skin condition is recognised by patches of dry skin which may itch and/or become painful and weep. There are many different causes of this condition, e.g. allergic reactions or stress. Normal salon services can be carried out, but if the condition is near the hairline, extra care must be taken. The client must be referred for medical treatment.

Psoriasis

This condition is caused by the overproduction of cells in the epidermis. On the scalp there are red patches which are covered by silvery-white scales. This condition is hereditary but can be brought on by emotional stress. Normal salon services can be given but extra care is needed. Refer the client for medical treatment.

Definition

Epidermis: Outer layer of the skin.

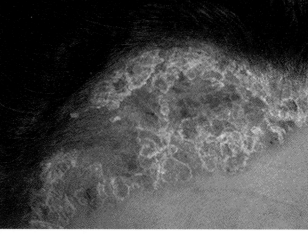

Figure 3.33 Eczema

Figure 3.34 Psoriasis

Online activity 3.5 WWW

Check it

Ingrowing hair

This condition occurs when a hair curls around and grows back into itself or the skin. Recognised by a raised inflamed spot. It may or may not be infected. It can be caused by the hair lying against its natural fall through friction, e.g. clothing rubbing against the skin. If the ingrowing hair is on the scalp, do not carry out salon services. The client should be referred for medical treatment.

Figure 3.35 Ingrowing hair

Alopecia (baldness)

Symptoms include a receding hairline, or balding on the top and the crown of a male head. There are several types of baldness.

Androgenic alopecia (male pattern baldness)

Androgenic alopecia starts with a receding hairline followed by thinning and may result in complete baldness. It is often hereditary. Normal salon services can be given.

Diffuse alopecia

Diffuse alopecia is a gradual thinning of the hair. Normal salon services can be given but medical advice should be sought.

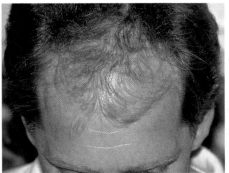

Figure 3.36 Receding hairline

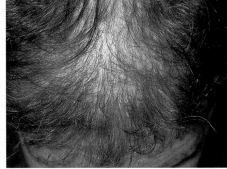

Figure 3.37 Thinning hair

Figure 3.38 Gradual thinning of the hair

Key information

Alopecia areata is hereditary but may be brought on by the client being stressed.

Alopecia areata

Alopecia areata starts as small circular patches of baldness, irregularly spread over the head. Causes are hereditary but it may be brought on by the client being stressed. This condition requires medical treatment.

Traction alopecia

Areas of hair loss caused by excessive pulling when styling hair. Tight plaits and braids can cause the hair to fall out at the root. Recommend that no tension is created on the hair for this service and the future until the hair has grown back. Then hair must be treated carefully to ensure the condition does not recur.

Cicatricial alopecia

Cicatricial alopecia is baldness caused by physical or chemical damage to the skin preventing hair from growing. Normal salon services can be given.

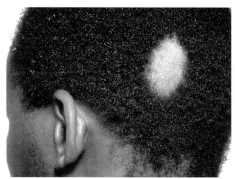

Figure 3.39 Circular patch of baldness

Figure 3.40 Tight plaiting can cause traction alopecia

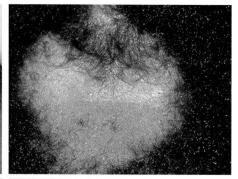

Figure 3.41 Cicatricial alopecia

Online activity 3.6 WWW

Check it

Sebaceous cyst

This is a small lump on the scalp or skin caused by a blockage of the sebaceous gland. Normal services can be given but this condition requires medical treatment.

Warts

These can be smooth or rough and are caused by a viral infection of the epidermis. The warts are non-contagious provided they are not damaged. Normal services can be given provided great care is taken.

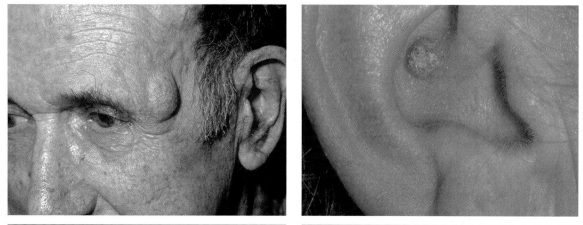

Figure 3.42 Sebaceous cyst on the face

Figure 3.43 Wart in the ear

Key information

Hairs go white when the pigmentation cells (melanocytes) do not function properly.

Safety first ⚠

The condition will need medical treatment. No service should be given to the client.

Definition 🔍

Fungi: Parasitic organisms that do not contain chlorophyll. Includes mushrooms and yeast.

Canities (grey hair)

Hairs go white when the pigmentation cells (melanocytes) do not function properly. The greyness is a mixture of white and coloured hairs. Shock can cause coloured hairs to fall out. The hair of the client can be tinted.

Contagious – folliculitis

With this disease the hair follicles become inflamed due to an infection. It may appear anywhere on the skin, not just on the scalp. The condition will need medical treatment. No service should be given to the client.

Tinea capitis (ringworm of the scalp)

Symptoms include a red ring which causes irritation to the client. It is a red circular rash with a white centre and brittle short hair in the patches. It is caused by a fungal infection and is contagious. This condition requires medical treatment. No service should be given.

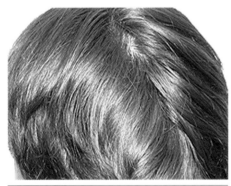

Figure 3.44 Grey hair

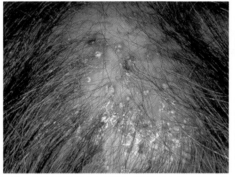

Figure 3.45 Folliculitis

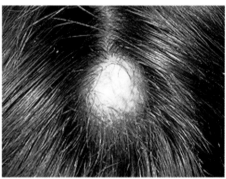

Figure 3.46 Ringworm of the scalp

Safety first ⚠

Impetigo is caused by a bacterial infection and can be transferred by using dirty towels.

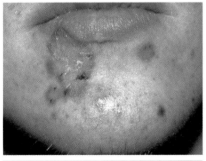

Figure 3.47 Impetigo around the mouth

Key information

How does the stylist know the difference between dandruff and lice? Dandruff will drop from the hair shaft but the head lice will slide up and down the hair shaft.

Impetigo

This condition starts as a red sore and then forms a yellow crust. It is caused by a bacterial infection and can be transferred by using dirty towels. This condition is highly contagious. It requires medical treatment. No salon service should be given.

Pediculosis capitis (head lice)

Infestations of head lice are fairly common. How does the stylist know the difference between dandruff and lice? The dandruff or skin flake will drop from the hair shaft but the head lice will slide up and down the hair shaft. Marks where the client has scratched may indicate the presence of head lice. Look for eggs attached to the hair shaft or insects that can be match-head size. The lice cling to a hair and feed on blood by biting into the scalp. Eggs are laid and cemented to the hair shaft. The condition is highly contagious by contact. Head lice are found in warm places on the head, at the nape and behind the ears. The condition requires medical treatment.

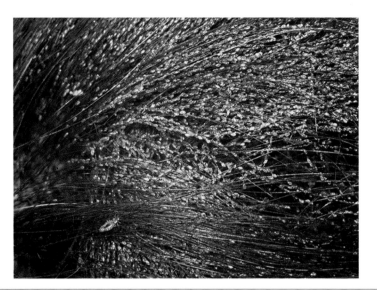

Figure 3.48 Head lice

Scabies

Scabies can be recognised as tiny raised and red lines on the skin. It is caused by an itch mite which burrows into the skin. It is highly infectious. No salon services should be given and the client should be referred for medical advice.

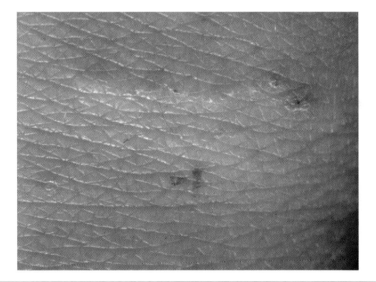

Figure 3.49 Scabies

Online activity 3.7 www

Drag into correct group

Hair growth patterns

The hairdresser should always try to work with the natural hair growth patterns. Do not try and force the hair into an unnatural direction. The hair growth patterns are classified as follows:

- widow's peak
- crown

- cowlick
- natural partings
- nape whorls

Figure 3.50 Widow's peak

A widow's peak is a very strong centre forward growth on the front hairline. It is best to avoid light fringes as they will lift and separate.

Figure 3.51 Crown

A crown is a circular movement of the hair (whorl) positioned towards the back, on the top of the head. It is important to identify the crown area because it can be a very strong movement. In some cases a double crown or two crowns are present, moving in different directions. Keeping length in the crown may help styling.

Figure 3.52 Cowlick

A cowlick is usually found on the front hairline across the forehead. The roots of the hair grow backwards and the mid-lengths and ends of the hair are forward, causing the hair to spring up. Cutting a straight fringe may be difficult as the hair tends to separate naturally. Moving the parting may help this.

Figure 3.53 Natural parting

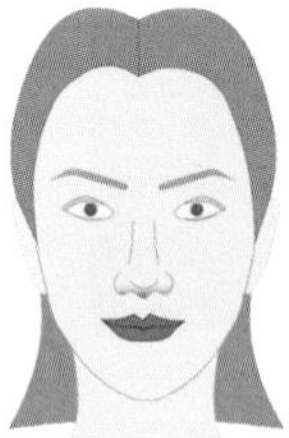

A natural parting is where the hair falls in a dividing line. It can be in the centre of the front sections, to the left or to the right. It is advisable to work with a natural parting and adapt any style. It is difficult to maintain a style that goes against a natural parting.

Figure 3.54 Nape whorl

Nape whorl describes the movement of the hair in the nape area which is below the occipital bone. They can be at one side or both sides. Styles are best kept very short or long.

Head and face shapes

The client may have the following head or face shape:

- oval
- round
- long
- square
- heart
- pear.

The oval shaped face is considered to be the perfect shape that suits any style. However, many people have differing features and it is therefore important to choose the hairstyle to suit both features and face shape.

Figure 3.55 An example of a round face

If your client has a round face, a hairstyle will be needed that is flat at the sides and high on the top. This will enhance the client's features.

Figure 3.56 An example of a narrow or long face

If the client has a narrow or long face, the hairstyle needs to be fuller at the sides and flatter on top.

Figure 3.57 An example of a square shaped face

If a client has a square or angular jawline, the hairstyle will need to be softer in style and covering part of that area. This will flatter the face.

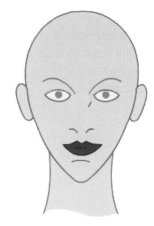

Figure 3.58 An example of a heart shaped face

A client with a heart shaped face will usually be very wide around the eyes and cheek-bones. They may also have a very wide forehead. A fringe would help to narrow the forehead and hair will need to be brought onto the face to create more fullness between the jaw and the bottom of the ear.

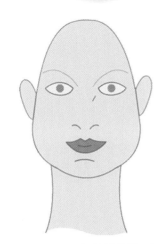

Figure 3.59 An example of a pear shaped face

If a client has a pear shaped face, the hairstyle will have to be flat around the jawline but have lots of volume and fullness around the temples. This will narrow the appearance of the face.

Figure 3.60 Large ears

Large ears that protrude need to be covered for a flattering effect.

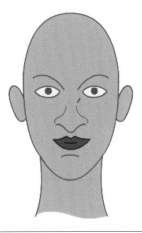

Figure 3.61 Large nose

If the client has a big nose or broken nose a centre parting will exaggerate this. Choose an asymmetric style. This will be more flattering.

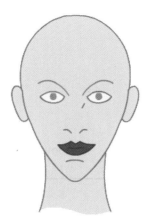

Figure 3.62 High forehead

A fringe will achieve the best effect for a client with a high forehead or receding hairline.

Figure 3.63 Short neck

A short stocky neck requires a softer hairstyle which is more flattering to the client.

WWW Online activity 3.8

Five in a row

Lifestyle

It is important that you create a style that is appropriate to the client's lifestyle and the way the client manages their hair at home or work.

Helping colleagues

Once you have Level 3 experience, you will find that colleagues will come to you for help with problems they have found during the diagnosis of their own clients. They may not have the experience themselves or they may not have the confidence to diagnose. Help out quickly and accurately without taking over, enabling them to return to their client and carry on with their diagnosis.

Figure 3.64 Help out colleagues quickly and accurately

3.3 Make recommendations to clients

As a result of the consultation, observations and tests, you must then recommend a course of action to be taken. This should be based on your thorough analysis carried out previously. Explain carefully the reasons for your recommendations. When making recommendations you should have an in-depth knowledge of all the products and services that your salon offers.

Key information

You should always explain carefully to your clients the reasons for your recommendation.

Current fashion trends

Keeping up to date with all the fashion trends will allow you to recommend a wide range of products and services. These trends change frequently. The following methods are ways to do this:

- exhibitions and trade shows
- trade magazines
- television
- courses
- websites.

Certain industries will lead the way in current trends. For example, music, film and fashion industries often have celebrities who update their hairstyles created for them by their stylist. These hairstyles will then be recreated around the world thus starting a trend.

Figure 3.65 Shows are a great way of keeping up to date with trends

Alternative services and products

If it is very unlikely that you will be able to achieve the client's wishes, then be truthful about this, explaining in a way the client will understand fully. For example, a negative skin test may not allow a certain colour to be applied to the hair. Explore all the other options with the client to achieve an outcome that they are happy with.

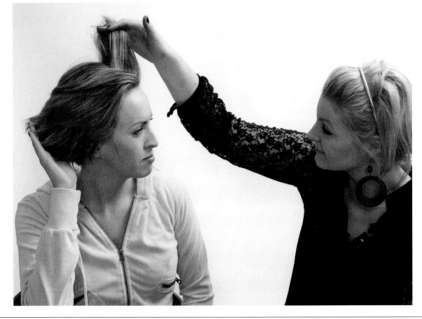

Figure 3.66 Explain fully if its not possible to carry out the client's wishes

Referrals to other salons

If a client wishes to have a service that your salon does not offer, follow your salon's procedures. Make sure that any salons you do recommend to the client have a high standard of service.

Figure 3.67 Follow salon procedure for referral to other salons

Referral to a pharmacist, GP or trichologist

You may need to refer the client to a pharmacist or general practitioner (GP). If you find a client has head lice, then refer them to a pharmacist. For other conditions clients will often be referred to their GP. He/she may then refer the client to a trichologist (specialist in hair and scalp conditions).

When referring a client be empathetic and supportive as some clients may become upset. Do not try to diagnose the client's problem, but rather suggest they see the specialist before visiting the salon again. If you think that a condition may be infectious, do not go into too much detail and be tactful when telling them this. Do not speak loudly and if necessary take them to a quiet area to ensure confidentiality is maintained.

Figure 3.68 Checking client's hair before referral

Figure 3.69 If you are referring a client, be supportive

Online activity 3.9

Five in a row

3.4 Advise clients on hair maintenance and management

When clients leave the salon, they want to feel they can recreate the style you have given them. This means that throughout the service you must give as much advice on all the techniques you perform and products that you use. To do this, you should:

- identify the client's current hair care routine
- suggest ways of improving current hair care routine
- give advice on products and equipment.

Identify the client's current hair care routine

Before advising on maintenance and management of their hair, it is essential you find out the client's current regime. This could be a very simple routine of washing and leaving to dry naturally. On the other hand the client may have a

Definitions

Empathetic: To understand and share the feelings of another person.

Diagnose: Identify the nature of a (medical) condition.

Infectious: Can be transmitted from person to person.

Confidentiality: To keep secret.

 **Key information**

Give your clients advice throughout the service.

Definition

Regime: A method or plan.

more complex routine of shampooing, conditioning and treating the hair using products and equipment to help with styling. Listen carefully whilst they explain their regime to you.

Figure 3.70 Ask the client about their current hair regime

Figure 3.71 Listen carefully to their response

Improving on the client's current routine

After you have found out the client's current routine, you should make your recommendations on how this can be improved. It is important that you advise the client on the best way to look after their hair. This could be recommending regular conditioning for hair that has a poor porosity, and regular visits to the salon for cutting to maintain the style. When making recommendations for improvement, any changes should not be too dramatic and should work with their budget, time and lifestyle.

Figure 3.72 Explain to the client how to improve their hair regime

Figure 3.73 Regular conditioning is the best way to look after hair

Products and heated styling equipment

When explaining to the client the use of heated styling equipment, take care giving health and safety advice. Continual use will damage the hair. Therefore regular conditioning and using heat protectors are advisable. Advise the client which products can be used at home. This should be based on the factors that influence the service. For example suitable products such as hairspray or mousse will help protect the hair from humidity. Ensure that your client understands all your advice before starting any service.

> ⚠️ **Safety first**
>
> Refer to Chapter 4 for more information on services and products.

Figure 3.74 Give advice on the use of heated styling equipment

Figure 3.75 Heat protectors will protect the hair during heated styling

Figure 3.76 Hairspray protects the hair from humidity

3.5 Agree services with your client

Once you have made your recommendations to the client you can confirm the arrangements by agreeing the following details with the client:

- how you or your salon will provide the treatment or service
- how long the service will take
- cost of the product or service
- appointment time.

Key information

Explaining as much as you can before the treatment starts will avoid any unexpected surprises. The time spent in the salon is to be a relaxing and peaceful time.

WWW   Online activity 3.10

Correct selection

Record keeping

Efficient record keeping cannot be overemphasised during the consultation and throughout the hairdressing service as it serves to ensure the safety of your clients, yourself and your colleagues at all times. Information should be full, accurate and clear. All records must be confidential and comply with the Data Protection Act.

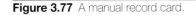

Figure 3.77 A manual record card.

Definition

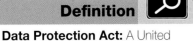

Data Protection Act: A United Kingdom Act of Parliament which defines UK law on the processing of data on identifiable living people. It is the main piece of legislation that governs the protection of personal data in the UK.

Legislation related to products and services

Always ensure the correct legislation is followed when agreeing products and services with your client:

- Trade Descriptions Act
- Sale of Goods Act and Sale of Supply Act
- Supply of Goods and Services Act
- Consumer Protection Act.

Refer to Chapter 4 to refresh your knowledge if necessary.

Figure 3.78 Ensure that you follow legislation when agreeing products or services

3.6 Worksheets

You can carry out the worksheets during your study of a chapter or unit, or at the end. An example is presented here and there are more online. If your college or company is registered with ATT Training, lots more are available. Write your answers directly in the book, but only if you own it of course – if it is a library or college book, use a separate piece of paper!

3.6.1 Current fashion trends

Keeping up to date with all fashion trends will allow you to recommend a wide range of products and services. These trends change frequently. Certain industries will lead the way in current trends. For example, music, film and fashion industries often have celebrities who update their hairstyles created for them by their stylist. These hairstyles will then be recreated around the world thus starting a trend.

Suggest some ways to keep up with current fashion trends:

_____

_____

_____

_____

Can you think of any current celebrity hair trends? Make a note of them here (remembering to record the date for future reference!):

_____

_____

_____

_____

3.7 Assessment

Well done! If you have studied all the content of this unit you may be ready to test your knowledge.

Check out the 'Preparing for assessments' section in Chapter 1 if you have not already done so, and always remember:

- You can only do your best if you have. . .
  - ○ studied hard
  - ○ completed the activities
  - ○ completed the worksheets
  - ○ practised, practised, practised
  - ○ and then revised!

 Now carry out the online multiple-choice quiz

. . . and good luck in the final exam, which will be arranged by your tutor/assessor.

Promote additional services or products

This chapter covers the NVQ/SVQ unit G18, Promote additional services or products to clients.

Promoting products and services not only makes for greater revenue for your salon but it also helps to keep the client's hair in the best possible condition after services have been carried out, for example colouring.

In this chapter you will learn about:

- identifying additional products or services that are available

- informing clients about additional products or services

- gaining client commitment to using additional products or services.

www.atthairdressing.com

CHAPTER 4 PROMOTE ADDITIONAL SERVICES OR PRODUCTS: CONTENTS, SCREENS AND ACTIVITIES

Key:

Sections from the book are set in this colour

Screens available online are set in this colour

Online activity screens are set in this colour

Identify products or services

Introduction

Identify products or services

Listening to clients

Round the board

Opportunities to identify needs

Knowledge of products and services

Complaints

Five in a row

Legislation

The Consumer Protection Act (1987)

Sale of Goods Act

Supply of Goods and Services Act (1982)

Correct selection

Trades Descriptions Act

Inform clients about products or services

Introduction

Times to inform clients

Opportunities to inform clients of products and services

Other methods of promoting products and services

Check It

Giving information to clients 1

Giving information to clients 2

Gain client commitment

Introduction

Buying signs

Client showing no interest

Correct selection

Delivery of products

Booking additional services and record keeping

Worksheet – Booking additional services and record keeping

Online multiple choice quiz

4.1 Identify products or services

Before recommending a product or service to a client, make sure that it is suitable. If you give an incorrect recommendation, and the client has a reaction or feels it is unsuitable, it can have a very negative effect upon the reputation of yourself or your salon. Therefore be quick to pick up on each individual client's needs and be aware of the legislation regarding products and services that your salon offers.

Key information

If you give an incorrect recommendation, and the client has a reaction or feels it is unsuitable, it can have a very negative effect upon the reputation of yourself or your salon.

Figure 4.1 Use your communication skills to find out what the client needs or wants

Listening to clients

This is the perfect way of establishing your client's needs in order to identify whether they may need additional products or services. During the consultation, use your communication skills to find out from your client how they currently style their hair and whether they use certain products.

Online activity 4.1 **WWW**

Round the board

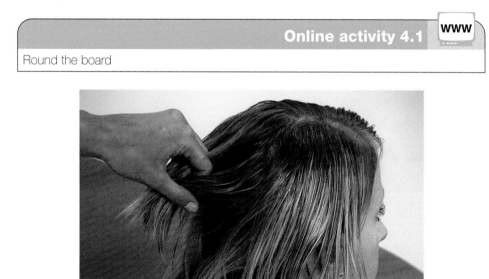

Figure 4.2 Oily hair calls for a suitable shampoo which you can recommend

There are many more opportunities other than during the consultation where you can identify clients' needs regarding products or services. For example you may be shampooing a client's hair and you notice that the hair is particularly oily. You could then recommend a suitable shampoo and/or conditioner that would help this and also styling products that would be suitable. It is important to gauge your client's reaction when suggesting products or services. The client may show interest through facial expressions or they may ask you about a particular product from which you could then give advice.

Knowledge of products and services

Make sure you know what your salon can offer your clients. It is important to have a thorough knowledge of all the services, products and the costs. This includes the features and benefits. If you do not know much about a particular product or service that your salon offers, make sure you ask another member of staff.

Make sure that any information regarding the products and services is kept updated. Many salons have times when a product representative comes to the salon to give information about new products that will be in the salon. Make sure that you attend these but if you miss them for any reason, ask other members of staff about the products.

Figure 4.3 Have good knowledge of all products

Complaints

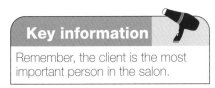
If a client has a complaint, always be polite, stay calm and remain courteous at all times. Never be argumentative, rude or contradictory. Remember, the client is the most important person in the salon. Inform the supervisor, e.g. stylist or manageress. They have sufficient experience and authority to decide on an appropriate course of action.

Online activity 4.2

Five in a row

Legislation

You must be aware of the following legislation when promoting products or services to clients:

- The Consumer Protection Act (1987)
- Sale of Goods Act (1979) and the Sale and Supply of Goods Act (1994)
- Supply of Goods and Services Act (1982)
- Trades Descriptions Act (1968).

Definition

Legislation: A law.

The Consumer Protection Act (1987)

This Act protects the buyer's safety from products by following European directives. This means that there must be clear information on the use of the product. Your salon must only sell products from a reputable supplier. Make sure that they remain in good condition whilst in your salon.

Figure 4.4 Ensure that the client has clear information about the product

Sale of Goods Act (1979) and the Sale and Supply of Goods Act (1994)

These Acts state that:

- products sold must be fit for the purpose stated and be able to do what they claim
- products sold must be of good quality.

Consumers can reject the products if they do not meet these requirements and have a refund as long as it is done within a set time.

Figure 4.5 Products must be fit for the purpose stated

Supply of Goods and Services Act (1982)

This states that services must be:

- at a price that is reasonable
- provided within a timescale that is reasonable
- given with reasonable skill and care.

Goods provided within this service must be:

- of satisfactory quality
- fit for their purpose
- as described.

Figure 4.6 Services must comply with the Sale of Goods Act

Figure 4.7 Goods must comply with the Sale of Goods Act

Online activity 4.3   **www**

Correct selection

Trades Descriptions Act (1968)

This states products must:

- be labelled correctly
- be labelled so as not to mislead the buyer
- state what the product is used for
- show the ingredients
- state where they were made
- be clearly priced.

All product information in writing and verbal recommendations must be accurate.

Figure 4.8 Product information must be accurate

4.2 Inform clients about products or services

Once you have gained enough information about the products and services and identified your client's needs, you now need to judge the correct time to communicate this information. Timing is most important as if you choose an inappropriate time, it can have very negative consequences. You do not want to annoy the client as you want them to visit your salon again.

 **Key information**

Timing is most important as if you choose an inappropriate time, it can have very negative consequences.

Figure 4.9 Choose a suitable time to communicate

Times to inform clients

Timing of communicating information about products or services is important. Judging your client's body language will help you to decide when this should be. For example if a client looks annoyed, then it is not a good time. A time that would be appropriate is when they look calm and they have enough time to think about what you have just advised.

Figure 4.10 This client looks annoyed so now is not a good time

Opportunities to inform clients of products and services

These include, when the client is:

- waiting for a treatment
- having their consultation
- having their hair shampooed
- having their treatment
- paying for treatment.

But remember to do this only if the client's body language and mood are positive.

Other methods of promoting products and services

These include the following:

- visual aids
- posters
- newsletters
- promotional flyers
- vouchers
- mailing out information.

It is important to show lots of enthusiasm about products and services that you are promoting.

Key information

But remember to only do this if the client's body language and mood are positive.

Figure 4.11 Brochures are a good way of promoting products and services

Definition

Promotional: To advertise or publicise.

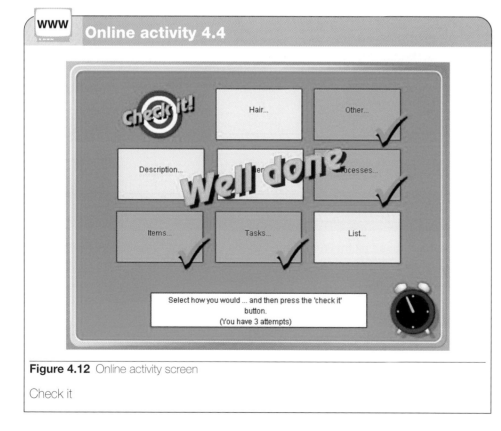

WWW Online activity 4.4

Figure 4.12 Online activity screen

Check it

4

Figure 4.13 Be honest about the products that you are recommending

---

Definition 🔍

Misconception: To have a wrong impression.

Giving information to clients

Information must be given to clients accurately and must not be confusing. Be honest and explain how the product or service will benefit the client. Let the client take a look at the product that they may wish to buy. Then show the client how to use it through a demonstration explaining how it will benefit them.

Give timings of treatments correctly so the client is not under any misconception as to how long it will take. If you give inaccurate information here, clients will not believe you in the future. Price lists should be shown clearly and the prices of treatments should have no hidden extras. Make sure the client is aware of vouchers that they could buy for friends and family. If there are any offers at a particular time, you should always know about these in order for you to promote them.

Figure 4.14 Timings of treatments should be given accurately

4.3 Gain client commitment

Once you have given all the information to the client, you should give them time to decide whether they wish to buy. You can usually pick up on signs to show that they seem interested.

Buying signs

A client is likely to buy if they:

- show positive body language, e.g. are nodding or smiling
- want to know more about the product
- smell or touch the product
- want to try the product
- want to know the price of the product
- want know how the product works.

Figure 4.15 This client is touching the product so it's likely she is interested in buying it

Client showing no interest

If a client is not interested in additional products or services they will:

- tell you that they are not interested
- start a conversation about another matter
- be interested in other activities in the salon.

Figure 4.16 This client does not look interested

If this is the case then check that you are giving the client the correct information and that you are explaining yourself correctly. It may be that you are giving too much information or that you are giving it at the wrong time. Try another way of giving information but don't carry on if your client still does not show any interest. Change the conversation to a subject that you know your client will be interested in.

Figure 4.17 Change the conversation to something you know the client is interested in

WWW **Online activity 4.5**

Correct selection

Delivery of products

The delivery details must be explained carefully to the client. If anything is unclear, run through the details carefully, repeating any information that you feel the client is confused about. If the client has to wait for their product then you should tell them for how long. Ring up the supplier or wholesaler directly if there are any problems with the client's delivery. Give clients information about this as soon as possible. Always ask your manager or supervisor if you do not feel you have adequate knowledge about a product or service.

Figure 4.18 Speak to your supervisor if you are unsure about anything

Booking additional services and record keeping

If the client wishes to book additional services, do this straight away at a time that is convenient to them. Always record details of products or additional services that the client buys or books.

Figure 4.19 Book additional services straight away

WORKSHEETS

4.4 Worksheets

You can carry out the worksheets during your study of a chapter or unit, or at the end. An example is presented here and there are more online. If your college or company is registered with ATT Training, lots more are available. Write your answers directly in the book, but only if you own it of course – if it is a library or college book, use a separate piece of paper!

4.4.1 Booking additional services and record keeping

If the client wishes to book additional services, do this straight away at a time that is convenient to them. Always record details of products or additional services that the client buys or books.

Write a detailed description of the process that you would go through to book an additional service for a client.

1. When the client is paying, ask if they would like book a new appointment. If so, would they like the same service?

2. _____

3. _____

4. _____

5. _____

6. _____

7. _____

8. _____

4.5 Assessment

Well done! If you have studied all the content of this unit you may be ready to test your knowledge.

Check out the 'Preparing for assessments' section in Chapter 1 if you have not already done so, and always remember:

- You can only do your best if you have. . .
  - studied hard
  - completed the activities
  - completed the worksheets
  - practised, practised, practised
  - and then revised!

Now carry out the online multiple-choice quiz **?**

. . . and good luck in the final exam, which will be arranged by your tutor/assessor.

Client services

This chapter covers the NVQ/SVQ unit G19, *Support client service improvement.*

The hairdressing industry is known for its excellent client service. This is due to the client being the focus of the business. There is also a great deal of competition in the hairdressing industry so it is very important to always think of ways in which your salon can improve its service.

In this chapter you will learn about:

- using feedback to identify potential client service improvements
- implementing changes in client service
- assisting with the evaluation of changes in client service.

CHAPTER 5 CLIENT SERVICES: CONTENTS, SCREENS AND ACTIVITIES

Key:
Sections from the book are set in this colour
Screens available online are set in this colour
Online activity screens are set in this colour

Using feedback to identify potential client service improvements

Introduction
Gathering feedback
Correct selection
Gaining information from your client during service
Client surveys 1

Client surveys 2
Client suggestion box
Salon website
Round the board
Using information to identify improvements
Possible updates to be made

Implementation of changes

Introduction
Identifying improvements to your products and services
Legal requirements
Correct selection

Presenting your ideas
Keeping staff informed when implementing changes
Targets and team working

Assist with the evaluation of changes

Introduction
Evaluation of changes
Round the board
Client feedback

Negative feedback
Worksheet – Client surveys
Online multiple choice quiz

5.1 Using feedback to identify potential client service improvements

Feedback from clients is essential to help you to improve the service you give to your clients. You may wish to gather information regarding the following:

- products
- services
- prices
- salon facilities
- client satisfaction.

Gathering feedback

Customer feedback is essential for you to gain the information needed to improve your service. Feedback includes:

- gaining information from your client during the service
- client surveys
- client suggestion box
- salon website.

Figure 5.1 Feedback can be gained during the service

Figure 5.2 You may ask your client to fill in a survey to find out their opinion

> **www** **Online activity 5.1**
>
> Correct selection

Gaining information from your client during service

Most of your feedback will be gained talking to your client during their hairdressing service. This time is useful for asking questions using effective verbal communication skills to gain invaluable information. Your client's body language and facial expressions can give away how they feel about certain issues. For example you may be talking about a particular product and even though the client does not verbally express their feelings, the look on their face will give it away. This is non-verbal communication and you must be able to pick up signs on a daily basis in order for you to improve the service and products offered.

>
>
> **Key information**
>
> Your client's body language and facial expressions can give away how they feel about certain issues.

Figure 5.3 Most feedback is gained from talking to your client during their service

Client surveys

>
>
> **Definitions**
>
> **Closed question:** A question that generates a yes or no answer.
>
> **Open question:** A question used to allow respondent to expand on their answer.
>
> **Multiple-choice question:** A question which requires the respondent to select the best answer from a list of choices.

Questionnaires can be used to collect information from your client. Planning is essential for an effective client survey. Include the dates you wish to start and finish and you should know what it is you wish to take from the survey before you draft it out. Think about the types of questions you wish to ask. Closed questions include showing a yes/no answer. However, these types of questions may not give you enough feedback as they can be limiting. If you include an open question afterwards, you may find out reasons why they feel that way. Multiple choice questions as shown will help to quantify the data, making the areas you need to improve on stand out clearly.

Questionnaire

The Hair Salon

Stylist's name:
Shampooist's name:
Date of visit:

1. Why did you choose The Hair Salon?

Advert	☐	Friend recommended	☐
Internet	☐	Yellow pages	☐
Other	☐		
Please specify: _____			

2. Reception welcome

Poor	☐	Good	☐	Excellent	☐

3. Interior of salon

Poor	☐	Good	☐	Excellent	☐

4. Consultation from stylist

Poor	☐	Good	☐	Excellent	☐

5. Atmosphere inside salon

Poor	☐	Good	☐	Excellent	☐

6. Shampoo and massage

Poor	☐	Good	☐	Excellent	☐

7. Team appearance

Poor	☐	Good	☐	Excellent	☐

8. Service quality

Poor	☐	Good	☐	Excellent	☐

9. Are there any areas you feel we could improve our service to you?

_____

10. Would you visit our salon again?

Yes	☐	No	☐

If no, please say why. _____

Thank you for taking the time to fill in this questionnaire. We appreciate your feedback.

Figure 5.4 Example of a questionnaire.

Think about where you wish clients to fill in the questionnaires. You could present one to complete in the salon, to take away with them, or you could post them on your website. If the questionnaires are anonymous it may enable the client to be more truthful about their feelings. Ensure there is a member of staff who is responsible for administrating the questionnaires.

Figure 5.5 Think about where you would like your clients to fill in the questionnaire

Client suggestion box

This method of collecting information involves clients posting their comments into a suggestions box. The benefit to this method is that clients usually comment on their true feelings, enabling you to be aware of your customers' needs. However, the problem is that they may post comments that are varied, making it difficult to see a pattern that you can focus on for improvements.

Salon website

Giving clients an option to email their feedback on your salon website is an excellent method of gaining information. You can upload your questionnaires or simply give the client an option to email the salon directly.

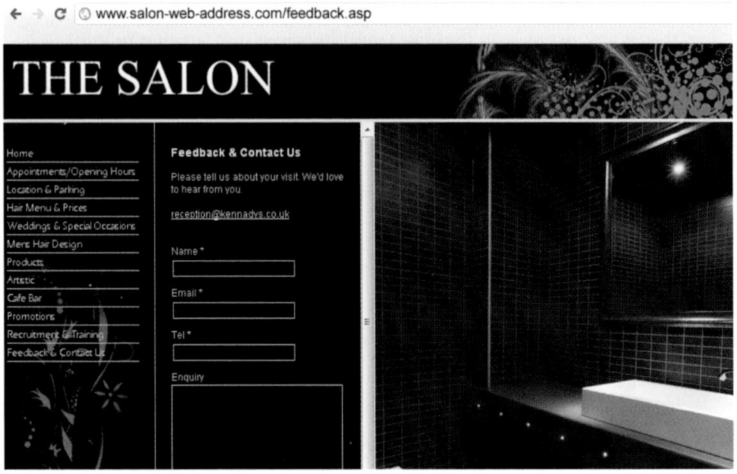

Figure 5.6 Feedback could be sent via the salon's website

Online activity 5.2 | WWW

Round the board

Using information to identify improvements

Once you have gained the information, you must then establish how you can make the improvements. The first method is to share the information with others. You can then decide as a team the best way forward.

If you have carried out surveys, you can look at the figures and see the areas that will need improving directly. You must look at the results and decide whether the survey gives you the information you were after.

Figure 5.7 Share your information with the team

Possible updates to be made

Your feedback may suggest that you need to update the following:

- product prices
- product range
- service price
- service range
- offers
- staff/customer service skills
- facilities
- staff motivation.

Figure 5.8 Feedback may show that you need to . . .

Figure 5.9 . . . update your facilities

5.2 Implementation of changes

It is essential to implement changes to improve the service that you salon gives clients. The previous section covered methods of gaining feedback from clients, but you should also be aware of changes that need to be made yourself.

Identifying improvements to your products and services

Identify any areas that you feel you or your salon could improve on. This could include:

- prices
- range of services
- presentation of staff
- standard of consultation
- standard of work
- standard of aftercare
- range of products
- refreshments offered.

Figure 5.10 You could improve your product range

Legal requirements

Keep in mind at all times the following legislation when implementing any changes:

- Health and Safety at Work etc. Act
- Data Protection Act
- Consumer Protection Act
- Sale of Goods Act.

These Acts have been covered in Chapters 2 and 4. Refer to them if necessary.

Key information

It is essential to promote equal opportunities at all times. There are Acts in place to enforce this including the Disability Discrimination Act.

Online activity 5.3 **WWW**

Correct selection

Presenting your ideas

When you have an idea for change in a specific area, you will need to present it to the appropriate person/s. This could be another member of staff or management, but whoever it is, use your communication skills to ensure that they gain a clear understanding of your proposals. Listen carefully to their thoughts on the matter. Do not interrupt them and ensure you are expressing positive body language.

Figure 5.11 Ensure you are expressing positive body language

Keeping staff informed when implementing changes

Once a decision has been made regarding changes, all staff and clients must be informed of what these will be. There are different methods of doing this including:

- discussion on an individual basis
- team meetings

- leaflets
- posters
- advertising through media
- salon website.

Figure 5.12 You can discuss decisions during team meetings

Targets and team working

If an objective of the salon is to increase productivity then a way of doing this is to set targets. If realistic targets are set then this can motivate all staff to achieve them. Whilst working as a team on improving the service your salon gives, make sure that everyone remains positive about the changes. This will increase the likelihood of clients being enthusiastic rather than feeling doubts about the changes that are to be implemented.

5.3 Assist with the evaluation of changes

Once the changes to client services have been implemented, they must be reviewed. You may have made changes to services that might not have benefited the salon's image; in actual fact clients may not like the changes made. This could have disastrous effects if your unhappy clients decide to move to another salon. Therefore to review the changes made is of key importance to yourself and your salon.

Evaluation of changes

Ensure that you have regular meetings with your staff to ensure that the changes that have been implemented are working. This will enable you to gain everybody's opinion. Any problems can then be discussed and the course of action decided upon.

Online activity 5.4

Round the board

Client feedback

It is important to gain client feedback when the improvements have been made. This is to check that the changes are actually working. This will also enhance your client relationships by showing that you care what they think about the products and services you are providing.

Figure 5.13 Find out from the client whether expectations have been met

Negative feedback

If you experience negative feedback about a change that was your idea, do not take it personally. If it is constructive criticism it can be used to re-evaluate your idea. If it is not constructive, you must take it as such.

Definition

Constructive criticism: Criticism or advice that is intended to help or improve something.

WORKSHEETS

5.4 Worksheets

You can carry out the worksheets during your study of a chapter or unit, or at the end. An example is presented here and there are more online. If your college or company is registered with ATT Training, lots more are available. Write your answers directly in the book, but only if you own it of course – if it is a library or college book, use a separate piece of paper!

5.4.1 Client surveys

Questionnaires can be used to collect information from your client. Planning is essential for an effective client survey. Include the dates you wish to start and finish, and you should know what it is you wish to take from the survey before you draft it out. Think about the types of questions you wish to ask.

Fill in the table below:

Type of question	Advantages	Disadvantages

5.5 Assessment

Well done! If you have studied all the content of this unit you may be ready to test your knowledge.

Check out the 'Preparing for assessments' section in Chapter 1 if you have not already done so, and always remember:

- You can only do your best if you have. . .
  - studied hard
  - completed the activities
  - completed the worksheets
  - practised, practised, practised
  - and then revised!

Now carry out the online multiple-choice quiz **?**

. . . and good luck in the final exam, which will be arranged by your tutor/assessor.

Creatively cut hair

This chapter covers the NVQ/SVQ unit GH16, Creatively cut hair using a variety of techniques; and VRQ unit 304, Cut women's hair to create a variety of looks.

This chapter looks at the skills needed to cut hair using a combination of techniques. You will build upon the knowledge of basic cutting techniques that you already have, in order to enhance your ability to create new and fashionable haircuts. Designing haircuts is of the utmost importance as you will be creating styles for individual clients based upon relevant factors influencing this choice.

In this chapter you will learn about:

- maintaining effective and safe methods of working when cutting hair

- restyling women's hair

- providing aftercare advice.

CHAPTER 6 CREATIVELY CUT HAIR: CONTENTS, SCREENS AND ACTIVITIES

Key:

Sections from the book are set in this colour
Screens available online are set in this colour
Online activity screens are set in this colour

Working safely

Introduction
Preparing the client for a haircut
Positioning during cutting
Waste disposal
Tools and equipment
Scissors
Thinning scissors
Correct selection
Razors 1

Razors 2
Clippers
Towels and gowns
Establishing client's choice of cut
Analyse hair and scalp
Hair density, texture and length
Round the board
Hair elasticity
Contraindications

Restyling women's hair

Introduction
Cutting techniques
Club cutting
Freehand cutting
Thinning
Tapering
Scissor over comb
Clipper over comb
Cutting angles and guidelines
Point cutting/texturising
Correct selection
Cross-checking
Dealing with problems during cutting
Baseline shapes
Select correct box
Preparing your client's hair
Creating a combination of looks
Creating a graduated bob 1
Creating a graduated bob 2
Creating a graduated bob 3
Creating a graduated bob 4
Creating a graduated bob 5
Creating a graduated bob 6
Creating a graduated bob 7
Creating a graduated bob 8
Creating a graduated bob 9

Creating a graduated bob 10
Correct selection
Creating a graduated cut on long hair 1
Creating a graduated cut on long hair 2
Creating a graduated cut on long hair 3
Creating a graduated cut on long hair 4
Round the board
Creating an asymmetric cut 1
Creating an asymmetric cut 2
Creating an asymmetric cut 3
Creating an asymmetric cut 4
Creating an asymmetric cut 5
Scrambled words
Creating a disconnection cut on long hair 1
Creating a disconnection cut on long hair 2
Creating a disconnection cut on long hair 3
Creating a disconnected asymmetric cut on short hair 1
Creating a disconnected asymmetric cut on short hair 2
After cutting and client care
Round the board

Provide aftercare advice

Introduction
Using tools and equipment
Products

Worksheet – Establishing client's choice of cut
Online multiple choice quiz

6.1 Working safely

Safety is the key issue when cutting hair. The tools that you use must allow you to perform the haircut that the client wishes to have. Be careful not to damage your tools as you work. Chapter 2 covers more general health and safety working methods in more detail. Refer to this unit if necessary.

Preparing the client for a haircut

It is important to gown the client effectively prior to cutting the hair. This is to protect the client's clothes and to ensure that the client is comfortable. Hair cuttings are extremely prickly when they go down the back of the neck and can penetrate the skin causing an infection. Cuttings are also very difficult to remove from clothes. Do not have too much bulk from clothes and towels around the neck; this restricts the accuracy when cutting and in some cases the mobility of the client's neck.

Figure 6.1 Gown the client in the correct way

Positioning during cutting

Whilst cutting the client's hair, it is important for you to move around the client's head. However, the client's comfort should be considered at all times. Their back should be positioned right to the back of the chair and as flat as possible. They should have both feet on the footrest or the floor. Not only will this be a more comfortable position for the client but it also enables you to create a balanced hairstyle. Your own comfort during cutting should be considered as well. Check your posture is correct, ensuring that your client's seat is at the correct height for you to work. Ensure that your work area is tidy and free from clutter.

Figure 6.2 Poor posture will result in a poor quality cut

Figure 6.3 Correct positioning will ensure accurate tension

Waste disposal

After cutting always remember to sweep up the hair cuttings and dispose of them in the appropriate place.

Tools and equipment

Scissors

These come in a variety of materials such as stainless steel, with metal or plastic handles. They also come in a variety of designs and price. Picking scissors up and holding them is the best way to see if they are suitable. It is important that they feel comfortable. Scissors should always be clean and sharp. Before sterilising remember to remove all loose hairs.

Thinning scissors

These are scissors specifically designed for thinning the hair. They have one or possibly two blades that look like the teeth on a comb. The teeth of the blades are sharp and cut the hair. The gaps between the teeth just allow the hair to pass through without removing any hair at all. The size of the gap determines how much hair is removed.

Figure 6.4 Different types of scissors

Figure 6.5 Thinning scissors with one blade serrated

Figure 6.6 And with two blades serrated

Online activity 6.1 **www**

Correct selection

Razors

A safety razor is designed to prevent accidental cuts to the person using it or the client. The disadvantage of this type of razor is that it does not allow the stylist to clean or mark out the hairline as it will not cut hair against the skin. It is used on mid-lengths to ends for reducing length and volume. Razors have a disposable blade. Some razors have a protecting handle.

Figure 6.7 Safety razor

Razors can only be used on wet hair; when used on dry hair they tear and shred the cuticle leaving the cortex frayed and exposed. It is also uncomfortable for the client. When razoring or close clipping, the client should be made aware of the risk of ingrowing hairs. The action of the razor or clippers can sometimes cause the position of the hair follicle to change, resulting in the hair growing back into itself or the skin. It is more likely to occur with clients who have curly or wavy hair. Salons using razor blades must dispose of them in a container such as a sharps box.

> ⚠ **Safety first**
>
> All staff must be fully competent in these health and safety duties including promptly taking action to remove or reduce any risks there may be.

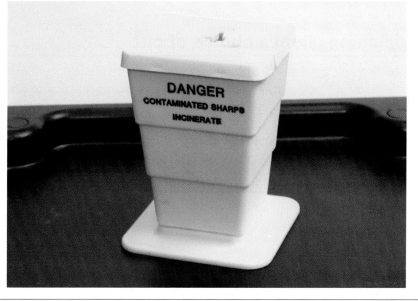

Figure 6.8 Dispose of razors in a box like this

> 🔍 **Definition**
>
> **Ingrowing hair:** A condition where the hair curls back or grows sideways into the skin.

Clippers

Electric clippers can be used with or without attachments. When in use the bottom blade remains still whilst the top blade moves across it very quickly to cut the hair. Do not use electric clippers with wet hands and remember to oil them using clipper oil after every use. When using electric clippers all repairs should be carried out by a qualified electrician.

Figure 6.9 Clippers

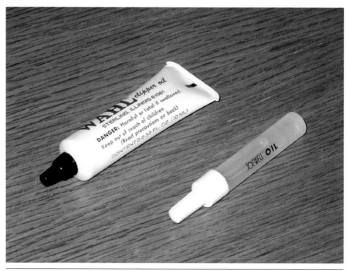

Figure 6.10 Clipper oil

Towels and gowns

All towels and gowns should be clean and sterile for each client to prevent cross-infection of parasitic, viral, fungal and bacterial diseases.

These include:

- pediculosis capitis
- herpes simplex
- tinea capitis
- impetigo.

Establishing client's choice of cut

Before cutting hair, a great way of establishing the client's choice of cut is to look through magazines or style books during the consultation. Look at what the client is wearing before they have their gown put on to identify their style. Ask questions related to their lifestyle. All information gathered at this stage will help you to establish a choice of cut.

Figure 6.11 Look through magazines or style books

Using your communication skills, recommend a style based on their preference and the relevant factors, e.g. face shape, growth patterns, current style, hair condition and type. Establish with the client the amount of hair to be cut. Always make sure that you repeat to the client what you understand to be their wishes. Confirm this once more before commencing the cut.

Figure 6.12 Use your communication skills to recommend a style

Analyse hair and scalp

Prior to all hairdressing tasks it is necessary to analyse the hair and scalp. This includes a visual examination and a physical examination. The natural hair-fall and the hair growth patterns are particularly important for you to be aware of before starting any haircut. Some growth patterns, face shapes and other factors may prevent you from cutting the hair in a particular style.

Figure 6.13 Analyse the hair and scalp

Hair density, texture and length

This will influence the way that the hair is cut. For example, if the client has very coarse and dense hair, they may need to have some bulk taken out by thinning or razoring. Alternatively if the client has sparse, fine hair, it should not really have much texturising to take hair away. The client's lifestyle may dictate how long or short the hair should be kept. For example it may need to be kept long enough to be tied back when required in a client's occupation.

Figure 6.14 Low density hair shown on the left, dense hair shown on the right

Online activity 6.2

Round the board

Key information

Hold wet hair with just a little tension to ensure that you don't cut too much off by mistake.

Hair elasticity

When cutting wet hair, if it is in poor condition (high elasticity) it will stretch more. Therefore hold the hair with just a little tension and be careful to not cut too much off by mistake.

Contraindications

During the analysis prior to cutting the hair other contraindications need to be taken into account. These can be divided into two distinct areas:

- infestations or infections including pediculosis capitis (head lice)
- tinea capitis (ringworm of the scalp).

Activity to complete www

Find out your expected service times for cutting hair and make a note here:

6.2 Restyling women's hair

In this section you will learn how to perform haircuts that include different techniques of cutting. You will be creating many different looks.

Cutting techniques

These include:

- club cutting
- freehand
- thinning
- tapering
- scissor over comb
- clipper over comb
- point cutting/texturising.

Figure 6.15 Club cutting

Club cutting

Each section of hair is cut straight across bluntly, usually done with scissors but can also be achieved with clippers. The hair mesh is cut straight across to produce level ends.

Figure 6.16 Freehand cutting

Freehand cutting

This is mainly used when creating a one-length look on straight hair. Comb the hair into place and then cut freehand without using tension on the hair. By not using tension on the hair when dry, it gives a better indication of where the hair will sit.

Figure 6.17 Thinning hair using thinning scissors

Thinning

Many cutting techniques can be used for thinning the hair, not just the use of thinning scissors. It can be carried out on wet or dry hair.

Figure 6.18 Tapering

Tapering

Involves a method of tapering the hair to remove bulk or volume alone, or to remove length and volume at the same time. Can also be known as feathering. The hair is cut to produce a tapered point.

Scissor over comb

Used when the hair is required to be very short and finely graduated. When using this cutting method a smooth flowing movement is required to avoid 'steps' in the hair. Keep the head up in a sitting position. Use the points of the scissors to lift a section of hair. Place a comb under the section of hair. Glide the comb in an upward direction. Follow the comb with the scissors and carefully cut the hair to the required length. Open and close the scissors rapidly clipping away at the length.

Figure 6.19 Scissor over comb technique

Clipper over comb

This eliminates the hard work from the scissor over comb technique. Place the comb and hold at the appropriate angle under a section of hair. Glide the clippers across the comb. Repeat this until the required length is achieved.

Figure 6.20 Clipper over comb technique

Point cutting/texturising

The points of the scissors are used to break up the point of the hair. This will create texture in hair that has been club cut. Another technique for texturing is called brick cutting.

Online activity 6.3 WWW

Correct selection

Figure 6.21 Point cutting

Cutting angles and guidelines

You should be aware of the cutting angles you are using throughout the haircut. The holding and cutting angle will affect the balance and amount of graduation it has. A guideline is the first section of hair that is cut and the next section/s are subsequently cut to. The number of guidelines will depend on how simple or complex the haircut is.

Key information

The holding and cutting angle will affect the balance and amount of graduation it has

Cross-checking

At the end of the haircut and possibly during, it is important to check the cut you have created. You do this by holding sections of hair out at right angles to the original sections. This enables you to see how accurate the cut is. If you find any areas that are not even, you can cut the hair accordingly.

Dealing with problems during cutting

If a thorough and accurate consultation is carried out, you shouldn't really make any cutting mistakes, but if you do then you should know how to deal with them.

An example of this is if you are cutting the hair and you find that there is a growth pattern that stops the hair from lying correctly. This should have been picked up from the consultation during analysis but to overcome the problem you should change the style to suit.

Another common problem that occurs is that you may feel that you have cut one side of a symmetric haircut too short. You should stop and check with your fingers, looking in the mirror at the same time. Only if the cut still seems out of balance, make adjustments as necessary.

Figure 6.22 Carrying out an accurate consultation should stop problems occurring during cutting

Baseline shapes

Baselines can be cut in a variety of ways including the following:

- symmetric
- asymmetric
- straight
- concave
- convex.

Symmetric – a balanced haircut that is even on each side.

Figure 6.23 Symmetric baseline

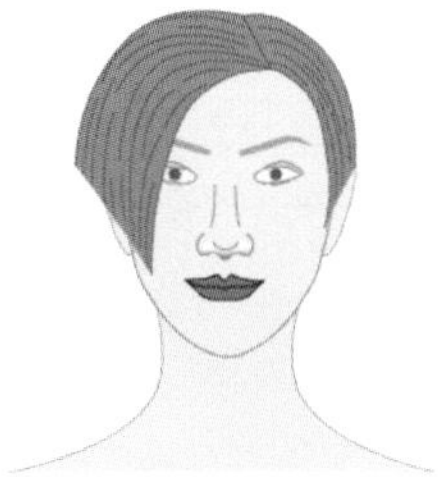

Figure 6.24 Asymmetric baseline

Asymmetric – a haircut that is uneven, e.g. with a side parting and more hair on one side than the other.

Figure 6.25 Straight baseline

Straight – a haircut with a straight baseline.

Figure 6.26 Concave baseline

Concave – the haircut has a baseline with a curve inwards or downwards.

Convex – The haircut has a baseline with a curve outwards or upwards.

Figure 6.27 Convex baseline

Online activity 6.4 **www**

Select correct box

Preparing your client's hair

Before cutting the hair should be clean. A build-up of products will only make the cutting service more difficult. Your assistant will shampoo and condition your client's hair prior to cutting. The shampoo and conditioner used should be specific to the client's type of hair.

Figure 6.28 Explain which shampoo and conditioner to use

Creating a combination of looks

You should be able to create a variety of looks using a combination of techniques including classic and current looks. A classic look will not age; an example is a bob. They do not go out of fashion. A current look is a look that is fashionable at the time. It is popular with people who change their hairstyle frequently.

The consultation that you have carried out with your client will establish which type of look your client wishes to have. Ensure that you consult with your client throughout the cutting service to check they are happy with the service.

Key information

Ensure that you consult with your client throughout the cutting service to check they are happy with the service.

Creating a graduated bob

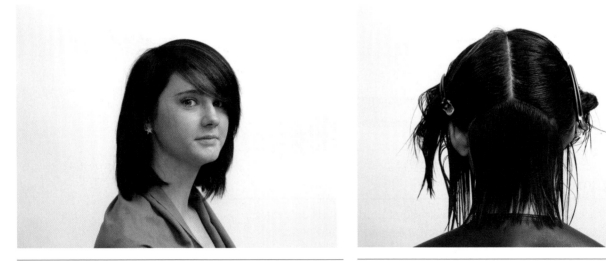

Figure 6.29 Before the service

Figure 6.30 Divide the hair into a hot cross bun effect

Figure 6.31 Take your first section of hair to be cut. Cut the first section to create your guideline

Figure 6.32 Cut the second section following the guideline

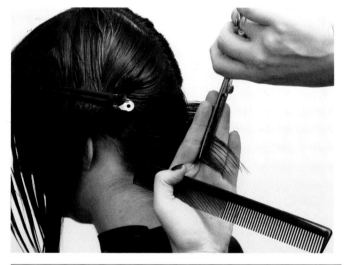

Figure 6.33 Continuing around the nape section blending long hair into short to create a steep graduation

Figure 6.34 Cut the baseline freehand to create a hard line for this style

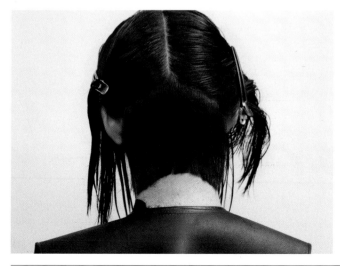

Figure 6.35 A hard line created

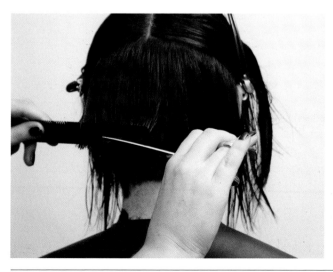

Figure 6.36 The scissor over comb technique is used to cut a tapered neckline into the style

Figure 6.37 Pull the hair down to check the length throughout the cut

Figure 6.38 When blending in the crown follow the guideline to create a steep graduation

Figure 6.39 Move on to the side sections and continue blending to create a longer length at the front. Point cutting will soften hard lines

Figure 6.40 This cut produces a longer length at the front

Figure 6.41 Dry and straighten the hair

Figure 6.42 Thin the hair using thinning scissors to remove bulk from the hair

Figure 6.43 Point cutting through the layers will soften the hard lines and create texture

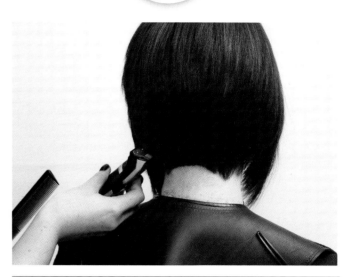

Figure 6.44 Creating a smooth line using clippers

Figure 6.45 A razor is used to define the outside line of the cut

Figure 6.46 The finished look: Blow-dry the hair into the style and apply relevant products to suit the hair

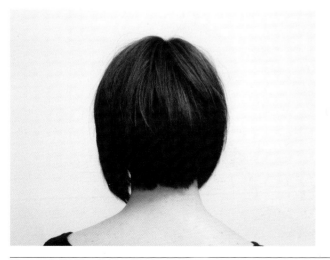

Figure 6.47 The finished look

The finished style incorporated the following techniques:

- graduation
- club cutting
- freehand
- scissor over comb
- thinning
- texturising.

WWW **Online activity 6.5**

Correct selection

Creating a graduated cut on long hair

Figure 6.48 This look starts with a V-section at the crown. Cutting this will establish the length of the cut, thereby creating a guideline

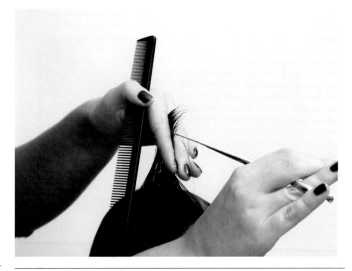

Figure 6.49 Cut the first section. Follow the guideline throughout the cut, from the crown blending into the longer lengths (online video)

Figure 6.50 Check the hair is cut evenly throughout

Figure 6.51 To finish, blow-dry the hair into the style and apply relevant products to suit the hair

The finished style incorporated the following techniques:

- graduation
- club cutting
- texturising.

Online activity 6.6   WWW

Round the board

Creating an asymmetric cut

Figure 6.52 Before the service

Figure 6.53 Divide the hair into a hot cross bun effect

Figure 6.54 Take your first section of hair to be cut as the guideline

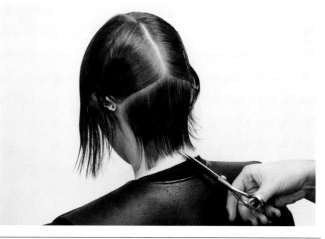

Figure 6.55 Cut freehand the asymmetric baseline

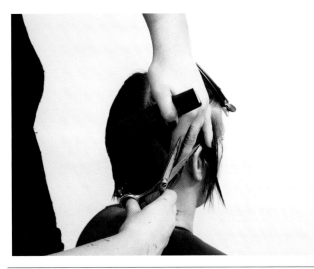

Figure 6.56 Starting at the short side of the asymmetric line, take small sections of hair, working towards the ear. Cut each section slightly shorter than the previous one

Figure 6.57 Move to the other side of the head, this time directing the hair back to create a longer length

Figure 6.58 Take sections of hair throughout the crown following the asymmetric line created. Blend the top layers in to create the finished length

Figure 6.59 The tapering technique can be used to encourage the hair to curl

Figure 6.60 Scrunch dry the hair into the style and apply relevant products to suit the hair to finish the look

The finished style incorporated the following techniques:

- graduation
- layering
- tapering
- club cutting
- freehand
- texturising.

Online activity 6.7 **www**

Scrambled words

Creating a disconnection cut on long hair

Figure 6.61 Before the service

Figure 6.62 Use a horseshoe method of sectioning the hair

Figure 6.63 Before cutting the top section, keep the longer hair separated. This can be done through twists or section clips

Figure 6.64 Cutting the first section to the desired length

Figure 6.65 Preparing to cut to the guideline. Follow the guideline through the crown section to create the chosen look. Continue this to the front area of the head

Figure 6.66 Crown sections cut to length

Figure 6.67 Front sections blended into crown length

Figure 6.68 Dry the hair. Use a comb to check the outline of the cut

Figure 6.69 Shaping outline of the haircut using the freehand technique

Figure 6.70 Texturising to remove unwanted bulk

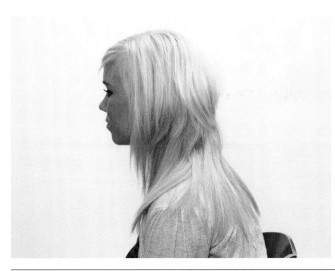

Figure 6.71 The finished disconnected haircut

Figure 6.72 The finished disconnected haircut

The finished style incorporated the following techniques:

- disconnecting
- club cutting
- layering
- freehand
- texturising.

Creating a disconnected asymmetric look on short hair

Figure 6.73 Before the service

Figure 6.74 The hair sectioned in the nape area in prepartion for the haircut

Figure 6.75 Position the comb at an angle to create an asymmetric line. Use a scissor over comb technique to remove the length

Figure 6.76 Dry the hair and continue the scissor over comb technique

Figure 6.77 Use the clipper over comb method at the side of the head

Figure 6.78 The clippers can be used to create a definite line to complement the style

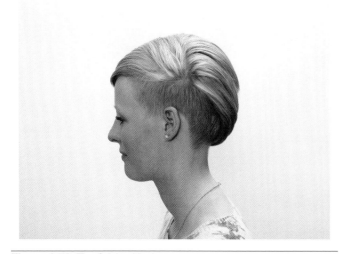

Figure 6.79 The finished look

The finished style incorporated the following techniques:

- disconnected
- scissor over comb
- clipper over comb.

After cutting and client care

When you have finished the cutting service, check the haircut all over for balance and make sure that you are happy with it. Look at the haircut from every angle. Once you are satisfied with the haircut remove any loose clippings of hair from the neck and/or shoulders. You can then dry the hair into the required shape. Ensure that the haircut you have created flatters your client's features. Check with the client that they are happy with the finished look.

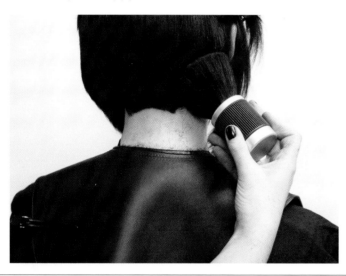

Key information

Ensure that you always look at the haircut from every angle.

Figure 6.80 Removing loose hairs from the back of the neck

Online activity 6.8   **www**

IE SENTENCES BY ENTERING

| After rinsing | the clients | hair they | should be |

_he ha_r

ask_d t_

o wra arou_d

CHEAT

s_t u_right

shoulde_s   fr_m th_ir   t_e towe_   shou_d remo_e   a_d y_u

YOUR ANSWER: asked

Figure 6.81 Online activity screen

Round the board

6.3 Provide aftercare advice

An important part of this service is to give the client aftercare advice. You should explain to the client how often they should return to the salon to maintain their haircut. This will depend on the length of the client's hair. For example, short hair may need to be cut more often than a long hairstyle.

Using tools and equipment

As you work, explain to the client how tools are used to create the look. For example, round brushes will give volume and curl whereas a flat brush will smooth straight hair. Explain to the client that continual use of heated styling equipment will damage the hair. Therefore regular conditioning and using heat protectors are advisable.

Figure 6.82 A round brush will give volume and curl

Figure 6.83 A flat brush will smooth the hair

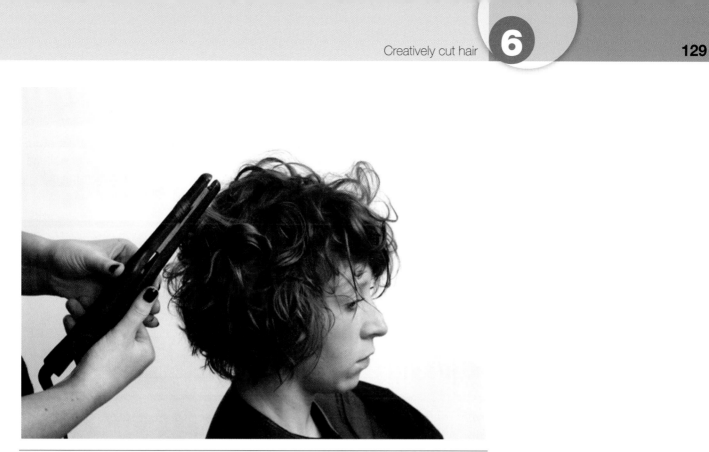

Figure 6.84 Frequent use of heated styling equipment will damage the hair

Products

Advise the client which products can be used at home. This should be based on the factors that influence the service. Refer to Chapter 4 for more information.

Figure 6.85 Giving the client advice

6.4 Worksheets

You can carry out the worksheets during your study of a chapter or unit, or at the end. An example is presented here and there are more online. If your college or company is registered with ATT Training, lots more are available. Write your answers directly in the book, but only if you own it of course – if it is a library or college book, use a separate piece of paper!

6.4.1 Establishing client's choice of cut

Before cutting hair, you will need to establish the client's choice of cut.

Name two items that may help you to do this during the consultation:

1. _____

2. _____

What can be an effective way to establish the client's current style?

_____

Suggest three questions that you might ask to help gain some information about the client's lifestyle:

1. _____

   _____

2. _____

   _____

3. _____

   _____

Using your communication skills, recommend a style based on their preference and the relevant factors. These factors include:

6.5 Assessment

Well done! If you have studied all the content of this unit you may be ready to test your knowledge.

Check out the 'Preparing for assessments' section in Chapter 1 if you have not already done so, and always remember:

- You can only do your best if you have. . .
  - ○ studied hard
  - ○ completed the activities
  - ○ completed the worksheets
  - ○ practised, practised, practised
  - ○ and then revised!

Now carry out the online multiple-choice quiz ?

. . . and good luck in the final exam, which will be arranged by your tutor/assessor.

Colour hair

This chapter covers the NVQ/SVQ unit GH17, Colour hair using a variety of techniques; and VRQ unit 306, Colour hair to create a variety of looks.

Colouring at Level 3 is not just about carrying out one technique but using a variety of techniques to get the desired effect. This effect will be based on each individual client. You will also be required to resolve basic colouring problems, e.g. restoring tone and depth and neutralising colours.

In this chapter you will learn about:

- maintaining effective and safe working methods when colouring hair and lightening hair
- preparing for colouring and lightening services
- creatively colouring and lightening hair
- lightening hair
- resolving basic colouring problems
- providing aftercare advice.

CHAPTER 7 COLOUR HAIR: CONTENTS, SCREENS AND ACTIVITIES

Key:

Sections from the book are set in this colour

Screens available online are set in this colour

Online activity screens are set in this colour

Working safely

Introduction
Personal protective equipment (PPE)
Protecting the client during the
colouring and lightening process

Posture and deportment
Roles of the salon assistant
Round the board
Record keeping

Prepare for colouring and lightening

Introduction
Understanding colour
The colour star
Correct selection
Natural colour
Choosing colour
Factors influencing colouring service
– condition of hair
Post-colouring treatments
Check it

Existing hair colour
White hair percentage
Processing time and temperature
Other influencing factors
Effect of artificial lighting
Correct selection
Tests
Contraindications
Preparing colouring products

Creatively colour and lighten hair

Introduction
Semi-permanent colour 1
Semi-permanent colour 2
Quasi-permanent colour 1
Quasi-permanent colour 2
Permanent colour
Diluting hydrogen peroxide
Five in a row

Recommendations
Different methods of colouring and
lightening effects
Check it
Block and slicing colouring techniques 1
Block and slicing colouring techniques 2
Block and slicing colouring techniques 3
Block and slicing colouring techniques 4

Lightening hair

Bleaching products 1
Bleaching products 2
Drag into correct order
Pre-lightening

Toning
Bleach application and removal
Full head lightener application 1
Full head lightener application 2

Resolve basic colouring problems

Introduction
Assessing the colour problem
Restoring depth and tone 1
Restoring depth and tone 2

Pre-pigmentation
Dealing with problems
Five in a row

Provide aftercare advice

Introduction
Time between appointments
Electrical equipment

Worksheet – Contraindications
Online multiple choice quiz

7.1 Working safely

Health and safety considerations during colouring and lightening are particularly important as you are applying chemicals that could be harmful to the client and/ or yourself.

You will have covered most of these key health and safety considerations specific to colouring when you completed your Level 2 training. We recommend that you refresh your knowledge if necessary. Also, refer to Chapter 2 for more general information on health and safety.

Personal protective equipment (PPE)

Ensure that you protect yourself by wearing the correct PPE during colouring. Permanent colouring products can cause dermatitis and wearing disposable gloves can prevent this. Drying your hands thoroughly and moisturising will also prevent this.

Figure 7.1 Dermatitis

> **Key information**
>
> Drying your hands thoroughly and moisturising will help to prevent dermatitis.

Protecting the client during the colouring and lightening process

Care should be taken not to allow colouring products to come in contact with the skin surrounding the scalp as this will stain. The client may also be sensitive to chemical products. A barrier cream can be used around the hairline and at the tops of the ears to prevent this happening.

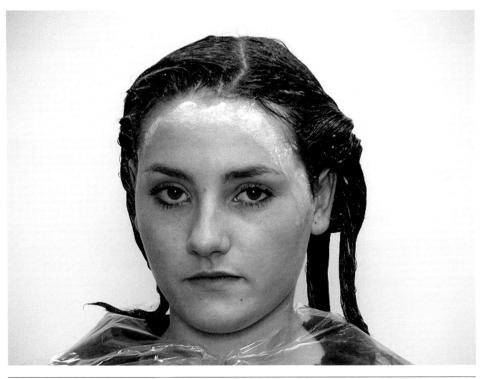

Figure 7.2 A barrier cream can be used to prevent colouring product coming in contact with skin

Key information

Colouring products stain, and bleach will remove colour from fabric, so it is important to protect the client's clothes from any damage through accidental spillage of products.

Definitions

Posture: The position of a person's body when sitting or standing.

Deportment: A person's behaviour or manner.

Since colouring products will stain, and bleach will remove colour from fabric, it is important to protect the client's clothes from any damage through accidental spillage of products. Make sure that the client is comfortable throughout the colouring process.

Posture and deportment

Make sure you check your posture during the colouring process to avoid injury. Your back should be kept straight, bend from the knees, feet apart with weight evenly distributed. If the spine is bent the back will have excess strain and the body will tire. The lungs will also be constricted; this lowers the intake of oxygen, which induces tiredness.

Role of the salon assistant

Before the colouring and lightening service, all products, tools and equipment should be prepared so that they are ready for use at the correct time. There may be a salon assistant who can help do this. Always give clear instructions to them. If you do not, you risk creating problems. To prevent this happening, you should ask the assistant to repeat back to you what you have asked them to do. This will clarify their understanding of the task. Ensure that your work area is clean and tidy at all times and that you are aware of product wastage. Used products should be disposed of in the correct manner.

Figure 7.3 Give clear and accurate instructions

Online activity 7.1 WWW

Round the board

Record keeping

It is important to record consultation details and information regarding all services carried out on a client including the following:

- date of skin test
- choice of colour
- date of last service
- documented evidence in case of litigation
- salon's professional image.

For this purpose all hairdressing salons have a system of client record keeping and the hairdresser must take great care in record entry.

Key information

All records must be confidential and comply with the Data Protection Act.

Activity to complete WWW

Find out your expected service times for colouring hair and make a note here:

7.2 Prepare for colouring and lightening

Preparation for colouring and lightening involves carrying out a thorough consultation to gain the correct information needed with regard to colour choice and the techniques used.

Chapter 3 covers consultation methods in more detail, including methods of testing and contraindications that may stop you from performing the service.

Figure 7.4 Visual aids will help you establish your colour choice

Understanding colour

White light is a mixture of colours. This is shown when rain falls on sunlight and a rainbow appears. In hairdressing you will need to distinguish the primary and secondary colours.

Figure 7.5 A rainbow produces a mixture of colours

The colour star

The achievement of a desired colour can be explained by the concept of a colour star. All colours are made up from the primary shades yellow, blue and red. Secondary shades are produced by mixing the primary shades together. Other colours can be made by mixing the primary and secondary colours together. The various possible colour combinations are achieved by varying the proportions of the primary and secondary colours.

Red, yellow and orange are the warm colours on the colour star.

Blue, green and violet are the cool colours.

Opposite colours on the colour star will neutralise each other. For example, if a colour appears to look too green it can be neutralised using a warm shade.

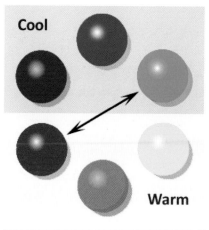

Figure 7.6 The colour star

> **Online activity 7.2** **www**
>
> Correct selection

Natural colour

Natural colour pigment in the hair is called melanin and is found in the cortex.

Pheomelanin is the red and yellow colour pigments.

Eumelanin is the black and brown pigments.

White hair is hair without pigment (colourless hair is called canities).

Grey hair is a mixture of natural coloured hair and white hair, often expressed as a percentage.

Colour depth is a term used to describe the natural lightness and darkness of the hair.

Choosing colour

When selecting a target colour, you must first use a shade chart to select the client's base colour. All shade charts use a system similar to the international coding system ICC (International Colour Code). Base colour describes the natural lightness and darkness of the hair (depth) and will be from 1 (black) to 10 (lightest blonde). This will be the first number on the chart. Any following numbers describe the tone of the colour.

Definitions

Pheomelanin: Natural pigment of hair causing a red/yellow hair colour.

Eumelanin: Black and brown pigments.

Canities: Pigmentation cells not functioning; hair turns white.

Key information

All shade charts use a system similar to the international coding system ICC (International Colour Code).

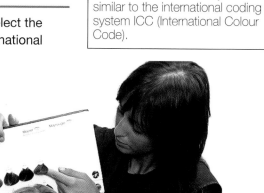

Figure 7.7 Checking the client's base colour

Factors influencing colouring service

Condition of hair

If hair is very porous, the cuticles will be wide open and therefore will easily take in colour. However, it will not be able to keep the colour for very long and so is likely to fade quickly. A pre-colouring treatment will help to improve the condition of the hair by strengthening the internal structure, allowing the hair to keep in more of the colour particles. Hair that is in good condition is likely to be resistant to colour. If this is the case, it can be pre-softened. This lifts the cuticle to allow the colour to penetrate the cortex. White hair can often be resistant to colour.

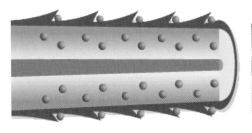

Figure 7.8 The cuticles are wide open and will easily take in colour

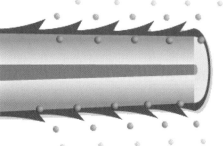

Figure 7.9 The colour particles will leave quickly, resulting in a faded colour

Post-colouring treatments

Figure 7.10 Examples of post-colouring treatments

Post-colouring treatments will:

- prevent colour fade
- prevent loss of moisture
- close cuticle
- restore hair pH.

www   Online activity 7.3

Check it

Existing hair colour

The client's current hair colour will affect the colouring service as it will determine the products and techniques that you use. For example, a client may choose a colour that lifts their colour by more than five shades. This means that you may need to advise the client to lighten their hair. Virgin hair will have different applications to hair that has been previously treated. Refer to the manufacturer's instructions at all times.

Figure 7.11 Client's existing hair colour will affect the service

White hair percentage

The amount (%) of white hair the client has will affect the type of colourant and hydrogen peroxide used. If the client wishes to cover all of the white hair a base shade must be used *with* the target shade. Table 7.1 shows guidance on the amounts of each shade to mix together but always check the manufacturer's instructions before preparing.

Table 7.1 White hair percentage

Amount of white hair	Ratio of base to target shade
25–50%	25% : 75%
50–75%	50% : 50%
75–100%	75% : 25%

Processing time and temperature

Processing time can be affected by temperature in the following ways:

- A warm salon will need less processing time than a cool salon.
- If the salon is cool then extra heat can be applied but check the manufacturer's instructions first before applying.
- Natural heat from the scalp may affect the development time; therefore it may be necessary to apply products to mid-lengths and ends before roots.

Figure 7.12 The temperature of the salon is an important factor

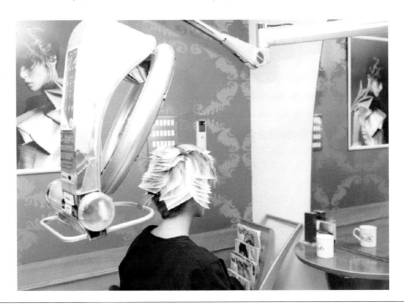

Figure 7.13 Applying heat to the head

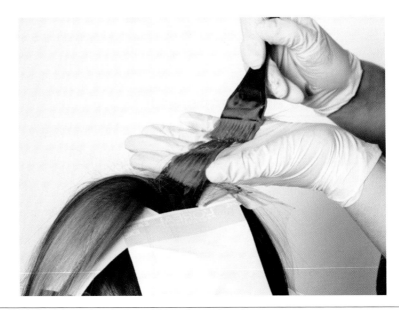

Figure 7.14 Applying colour to the mid-lengths and ends

Other influencing factors

Other factors that will affect the colouring service include:

- hair texture and density
- skin tone (warm or cool)
- haircut – must be balanced with colour
- facial features, e.g. eye colour
- length of hair
- career and lifestyle.

Effect of artificial lighting

When looking at colours in the salon, special consideration must to given to the type of lighting. Natural light shows off the true hair colour. A standard halogen bulb gives off a yellow colour but adds warmth to the hair and neutralises cool ash tones. Fluorescent tubes give off a bluish green light so hair appears less warm. A halogen or fluorescent type that gives off a warm white light may be the best for showing off colour in the correct depth and tone.

Figure 7.15 Consider the lighting in your salon

Online activity 7.4 **www**

Correct selection

Tests

Carry out the following colour tests:

- skin test
- hair porosity test
- hair elasticity test
- hair incompatibility test
- hair strand/colour test.

Record all results of these tests.

Contraindications

Any contraindications that you find will not allow you to carry out the colour service. These include:

- skin disorders
- damaged hair
- negative skin test
- sensitive scalp
- history of allergic reactions
- product incompatibility
- medical advice/instructions.

Figure 7.16 Check for contraindications

Preparing colouring products

Before preparing and/or mixing colour, always read the manufacturer's instructions carefully. Measure out products accurately, making sure you are aware of the correct volume of hydrogen peroxide to use. Always wear the correct PPE.

Safety first ⚠
Always wear the correct PPE when preparing colour.

Figure 7.17 Preparing colour

7.3 Creatively colour and lighten hair

This section is concerned with combining colouring and lightening techniques to create various effects. Before you begin, you must recommend the colour and technique that will be suitable for your individual client.

Semi-permanent colour

Small colour molecules are deposited in the hair cuticle or wedged under the open cuticle. Semi-permanent colours are collectively called nitro-dyes. The dyes will darken the hair, add strong colour tones, blend in white hair, and achieve a subtle colour change. The colour fades each time it is shampooed and lasts between 6 and 8 washes.

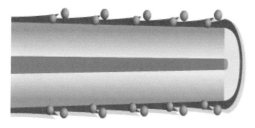

Figure 7.18 The colour molecules are deposited in the hair cuticle or wedged under the open cuticle

Quasi-permanent colour

Quasi-permanent lasts longer than a semi-permanent colour but not as long as a permanent tint. The colour molecules do not penetrate as far into the cortex as the permanent tint. Unlike the semi-permanent colour it fades over a longer period of time and will lighten, colour and tone the hair. Like with permanent tint there is usually a regrowth line.

Most quasi-colours are mixed with their own developers containing a low percentage of hydrogen peroxide. The colour molecules are oxidised by the oxygen from hydrogen peroxide.

Quasi-colours are popular because of the variety of fashion shades to choose from as well as natural shades. They are more effective and longer lasting than semi-permanent colours. They are not so harsh on the hair, add shine and contain conditioning properties.

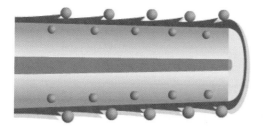

Figure 7.19 The colour molecules do not penetrate very far into the cortex

Permanent colour

With this type of colour the molecules penetrate the cuticle and are absorbed into the cortex. The colour molecules are oxidised by the hydrogen peroxide and remain permanently deposited in the cortex. Tint remains in the hair until it is cut out and will darken, add tone and lighten the hair. Hydrogen peroxide is required to be mixed with the tint in order to activate it.

Definition

Oxidation: The addition of oxygen.

On the basis of the choice of tint, the strength of hydrogen peroxide required is determined by whether the hair is to be tinted darker or lighter. In general hair being tinted lighter will require a peroxide of 30 volume (9%) while hair being tinted darker, or within its base colour depth, will require a strength of 20 volume (6%).

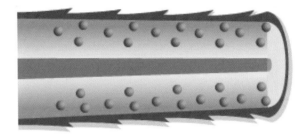

Figure 7.20 The molecules penetrate the cuticle and are absorbed into the cortex

Diluting hydrogen peroxide

Should you need to dilute hydrogen peroxide use water in the correct ratio shown in Table 7.2.

Table 7.2 Dilution of hydrogen peroxide

Current strength	Ratio water: peroxide	Dilutes to
20 vol (6%)	1:1	10 vol (3%)
30 vol (9%)	2:1	10 vol (3%)
30 vol (9%)	1:2	20 vol (6%)
40 vol (12%)	1:1	20 vol (6%)
40 vol (12%)	1:3	30 vol (9%)

www **Online activity 7.5**

Five in a row

Recommendations

Your recommendation to your client will be made after a full consultation has been carried out. To help you make your recommendations, visual aids should be used. Shade charts are extremely useful as they enable you to show the client the colours available to them.

Figure 7.21 Make recommendations after consultation

Different methods of colouring and lightening effects

These include:

- slicing
- block
- weaving.

Figure 7.22 Slicing application

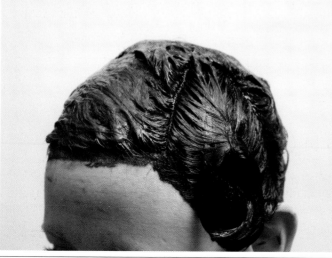

Figure 7.23 Block colour application

Figure 7.24 Weaving application

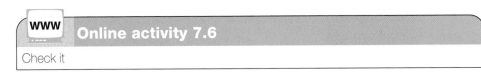

www **Online activity 7.6**

Check it

Block and slicing colouring techniques

Figure 7.25 To create the desired look on long hair, a lightening product is applied to the hair as a block colour giving a bold effect

Figure 7.26 To balance the look, the technique is carried out either side of the crown

Figure 7.27 After application of block colour

Figure 7.28 A packet is used as a barrier to avoid the colour spreading to the rest of the hair

Figure 7.29 Slices using permanent colour are applied to the front of the hair to break up the natural colour. This gives a subtle depth to the hair and complements the block colour. (online video). Packets have been used to create the slices in this example but foils could be used instead

Figure 7.30 Leave the hair to develop for the correct length of time

Figure 7.31 Rinse and shampoo the hair

Figure 7.32 Applying a toner to the lightened hair to remove unwanted gold tones

Figure 7.33 Stay with the client until the toner has reached the desired effect

Figure 7.34 Remove toner and condition the hair before styling as required

Figure 7.35 The finished look

Figure 7.36 The finished look

7.4 Lightening hair

Bleaching products

The two most commonly used types of bleaches are:

- powder bleach used for highlights (most powder bleaches are not recommended for use on the scalp)
- emulsion oil cream or gel bleach used for full head treatment.

Figure 7.37 Powder bleach

Figure 7.38 Emulsion oil cream or gel bleach

Safety first

Always take care not to inhale any powder bleach when dispensing it into the bowl.

High lifts are similar to bleach but kinder to the hair. They will only lift a few shades. In general hair being bleached will require a peroxide of 30 volume (9%). Ensure the manufacturer's instructions are followed when mixing up lighteners.

When bleach is mixed with hydrogen peroxide, oxygen is released. The product penetrates the cuticle and then the cortex. Oxygen mixes with the melanin in the cortex creating oxymelanin. This oxymelanin is colourless.

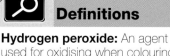

The oxygen forms with the different colour pigments in a certain order:

1. black
2. brown
3. red
4. orange
5. orange yellow
6. yellow
7. pale yellow

Bleach remains within the hair until it is cut out.

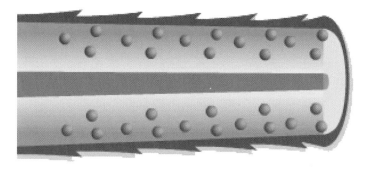

Figure 7.39 Bleach penetrates the cuticle and then the cortex

Online activity 7.7 www

Drag into correct order

Pre-lightening

If the required amount of lift cannot be achieved when lightening, then the hair can be pre-lightened. Bleach is used to do this but take great care; only lighten the hair to the same depth as the target shade. If you do not do this and you bleach more than you need do, this can damage the hair unnecessarily.

Toning

It may be necessary to remove the yellow tones from the hair after bleaching. Violet may be used to neutralise. If used, toner should be applied to damp hair, starting at the roots and working towards the mid-lengths and ends. The products should be used according to the manufacturer's instructions.

Bleach application and removal

Ensure when applying bleach products to the hair, that you carry out regular colour/strand and elasticity tests to check the development and condition of the hair.

The method of applying lightener to regrowth hair is the same as for applying tint to regrowth but take care that the lightener is not overlapping onto the hair that has previously been lightened. This will cause the hair to be oversensitised to the lightener.

When rinsing off, this must be done without massaging the hair and with water that is warm or tepid. Make sure that all product is rinsed from the hair. The hair

Figure 7.40 Violet may be used to neutralise yellow tones

should be washed and conditioned with an anti-oxidising conditioner treatment which will close the cuticle and keep the colour locked in.

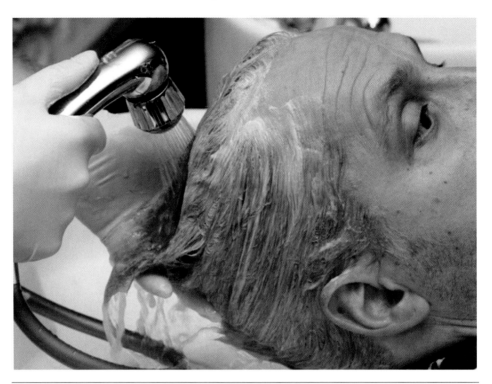

Figure 7.41 Rinse off bleach with water that is warm or tepid

Full head lightener application

Figure 7.42 Before the service

Figure 7.43 The hair is sectioned for ease of application

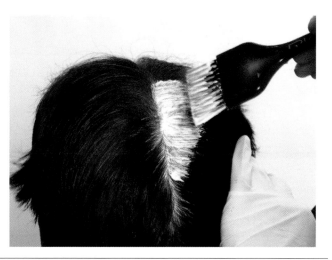

Figure 7.44 As the model will be having his hair cut after the service, the lightener is applied to the roots first. It is important to remember that if hair was kept this length the lightener would have been applied to mid-lengths and ends first and then the roots

Figure 7.45 Lightener applied all over the head. Leave to develop. Added heat may be applied but check the manufacturer's instructions before

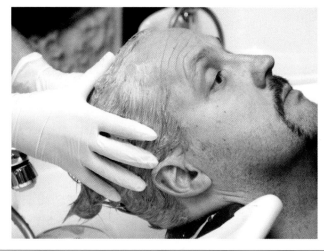

Figure 7.46 The bleach is rinsed off and a toner applied. Leave for full development. Shampoo and condition

Figure 7.47 The finished colour

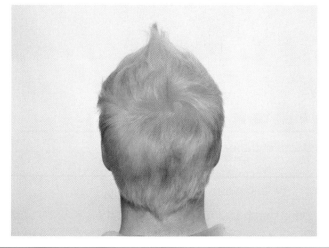

Figure 7.48 The finished colour

7.5 Resolve basic colouring problems

You should be able to resolve certain colouring and lightening problems in the salon. To do this, you should know why the problem has occurred in the first place.

This section covers restoring depth and tone, pre-pigmentation and general problems that may occur during colouring and lightening. Colouring resistant hair is covered under 'Prepare for colour and lightening' and neutralising colour tone is covered under 'Lightening hair'. Refer to these sections if necessary.

Assessing the colour problem

Make sure that you know exactly what the problem is by asking the client, using effective communication skills. Once you have established the problem, you should assess the client's hair. The options available to resolve the problem should be presented to the client in a thorough manner. The client can then make the decision on what course of action to take.

Figure 7.49 Present methods of resolving the colour problem

Restoring depth and tone

Reasons for losing colour depth and tone include:

- hair fading in sunlight
- hair is very porous due to overcolouring.

A common method of restoring depth and tone is to refresh the colour by adding the previous colour. If required, a pre-colouring treatment can be applied to even out the porosity of the hair.

Figure 7.50 This colour has faded

Figure 7.51 Application of pre-colour treatment if necessary

Figure 7.52 A permanent tint is applied to the hair and left to develop for full development time according to the manufacturer's instructions. Rinse, shampoo and condition the hair. Style as required

Figure 7.53 Depth and tone restored to the hair

Pre-pigmentation

If a client has bleached hair and wishes to re-colour to go back to a more natural darker shade, the first process is to carry out pre-pigmentation to add warmth, followed by the application of the target shade. As bleaching takes out the warm tones, which are red and yellow, these must be replaced before applying the target shade or else the hair will be a green colour.

 **Definition**

Pre-pigmentation: Adding a warm colour to the hair before applying the target shade.

Figure 7.54 Carrying out pre-pigmentation

Dealing with problems

Table 7.3 shows you what certain problems are caused by and what action you should take in the event of this happening. Study it carefully.

Table 7.3 Potential problems and how to deal with them

Problem	Caused by	Action to take
Stains on the skin	Applying too much product Sloppy application Failing to emulsify during removal	Use a stain remover
Poor hair condition	Colour left on for too long Incorrect strength of peroxide Unsuitable product used	Use a penetrating conditioning treatment to strengthen the hair
Over-processing of product	Incorrect strength of peroxide Product left on for too long	Use a penetrating conditioning treatment to strengthen the hair
Under-processing of product	Incorrect strength of peroxide Lack of product applied Product not left to develop for recommended time	Re-apply bleach or colour if the hair is strong enough
Patchy result	Application uneven Porosity uneven	Spot colour where appropriate
Seepage during highlighting	Foils and mesh incorrectly used Poor application of product	Spot colour where appropriate
Yellow overtones	Bleach not left on for long enough Incorrect product used Natural (base) hair too dark	Use a violet toner
Faded colour	Sunlight Porous hair	Cover hair during sun exposure A course of a restructuring conditioning treatment to strengthen the hair

www   **Online activity 7.8**

Five in a row

7.6 Provide aftercare advice

Throughout the colouring service, advise the client on the best products to use to maintain colour and condition. Also explain to the client what they should avoid as there are many products that can cause the colour to fade. The products that you recommend should also be based on the factors that influence the service, including career and lifestyle.

Refer to Chapter 4 for information on promoting products and services.

Time between appointments

You should explain to the client how often they should return to the salon to maintain their colour. This will depend on the type of colour. For example, a client who has had a full head colour should be advised to return to the salon after 4–5 weeks to have their regrowth coloured whereas those with highlights/lowlights could return after 2–4 months.

The time between appointments will also depend on the clients' wishes. Most clients will want to have their hair re-coloured once they start seeing regrowth.

Figure 7.55 Intervals between salon visits will . . .

Figure 7.56 . . .depend on colouring techniques that have been applied

Electrical equipment

When explaining to the client the use of heated styling equipment, take care giving health and safety advice. Continual use will damage the hair. Therefore regular conditioning and using heat protectors are advisable.

Safety first

Give clients health and safety advice about electrical equipment.

7.7 Worksheets

You can carry out the worksheets during your study of a chapter or unit, or at the end. An example is presented here and there are more online. If your college or company is registered with ATT Training, lots more are available. Write your answers directly in the book, but only if you own it of course – if it is a library or college book, use a separate piece of paper!

7.7.1 Contraindications

A contraindication may stop you from performing a service.

The table below lists some contraindications that you may come across. Fill in the empty boxes.

Contraindication	What signs might you see of the contraindication?
Skin disorders	
Hair with poor elasticity	
Hair with high porosity	
Negative skin test	
Sensitive scalp	
Product incompatibility	

7.8 Assessment

Well done! If you have studied all the content of this unit you may be ready to test your knowledge.

Check out the 'Preparing for assessments' section in Chapter 1 if you have not already done so, and always remember:

- You can only do your best if you have. . .
  - studied hard
  - completed the activities
  - completed the worksheets
  - practised, practised, practised
  - and then revised!

Now carry out the online multiple-choice quiz ❓

. . . and good luck in the final exam, which will be arranged by your tutor/assessor.

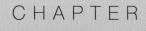

Colour correction

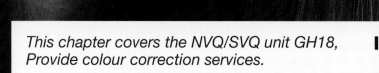

This chapter covers the NVQ/SVQ unit GH18, Provide colour correction services.

As colouring services are becoming more popular, there will be an increased need for correction. Colour correction is used to darken, lighten or change tone. This is a Level 3 unit, as each problem and the method of fixing it will be individual to each client. Advanced skills will be needed to analyse and correct each colouring problem that you come across.

In this chapter you will learn about:

■ maintaining effective and safe methods of working when correcting hair colour

■ determining the problem

■ planning and agreeing a course of action to correct the colour

■ correcting the colour

■ providing aftercare advice.

CHAPTER 8 COLOUR CORRECTION: CONTENTS, SCREENS AND ACTIVITIES

Key:
Sections from the book are set in this colour
Screens available online are set in this colour
Online activity screens are set in this colour

Working safely
Introduction

Determine the problem

Introduction   Colour correction problems
Consultation   Removing artificial hair colour
Round the board   Oxidation and reduction
Checking the client's records   Re-colouring hair after hair colour
Visually checking the client's hair and   reduction
scalp   Bands of colour
Tests   Bleached hair re-colouration
Contraindications   Highlight/lowlight correction
Correct selection   Five in a row

Plan and agree a course of action to correct colour

Introduction   Maintain the colour and future
Present suitable options   hairdressing services
Recommendations   Record the course of action
                                           Round the board

Correct colour

Introduction   Re-colouring hair that has had artificial
Preparing client's hair for colouring –   colour removed
pre-colouring   Drag into correct order
Pre-softening   Removing bands of colour
Processing time and temperature   Re-colouring bleached hair using pre-
Correct selection   pigmentation and permanent colour 1
Preparing colour correction products   Re-colouring bleached hair using pre-
Removing artificial colour using colour   pigmentation and permanent colour 2
reducers 1   Re-colouring bleached hair using pre-
Removing artificial colour using colour   pigmentation and permanent colour 3
reducers 2   Highlight and lowlight correction 1
Removing artificial colour using colour   Highlight and lowlight correction 2
reducers 3   Highlight and lowlight correction 3
                                           Shoot the target

Provide aftercare advice

Introduction   Worksheet – Remove artificial colour
Time between appointments   using colour reducers
Electrical equipment   Online multiple choice quiz

8.1 Working safely

This section's knowledge is covered in the previous chapter, 'Colour hair'. Refer to this if necessary. More general information with regard to health and safety is covered in Chapter 2.

Activity to complete www

Find out your expected service times for colour correction and make a note here:

8.2 Determine the problem

Before correcting the client's hair colour, it is very important to find out the reason *why* they have the problem. Once you know the reason, you can select the right method of correcting the colour using appropriate products. The following methods are used to determine the problem:

- consultation
- checking the client's records
- visually checking the client's hair and scalp
- carrying out relevant tests.

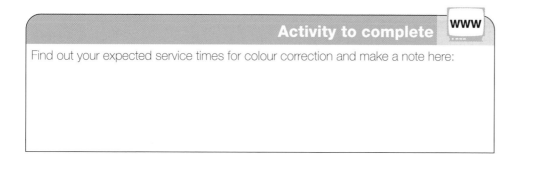

Key information

Refer to the previous chapter if you would like to refresh your knowledge on the colouring principles and the factors affecting the colouring service.

Consultation

The main method of establishing the client's colour problem is through a consultation. Use your communication skills to find out from the client exactly how the problem has occurred. Repeat back to them what the problem is, so that you can be sure you understand correctly.

Figure 8.1 Using communication skills to find out the problem

The consultation will require you to obtain information from the client such as details of previous treatments including dates they last applied colour to their hair. Find out whether they have contraindications to the colouring service.

Figure 8.2 Ask the client whether they have used previous treatments

The consultation will allow you to discuss and select a target shade and the products to use. Record all the client's responses.

Figure 8.3 Selecting a target shade

Chapter 3 covers consultation methods in more detail including methods of testing and contraindications that may stop you from performing the service.

WWW   **Online activity 8.1**

Round the board

Checking the client's records

After asking the client directly, check the client's records to see if they have had any previous allergic reactions to colouring products. These records may give you information about when they last applied colour to their hair if they cannot remember themselves.

Key information

To comply with the Data Protection Act, all records must be confidential.

Figure 8.4 Check the client's records

Visually check the client's hair and scalp

It is important to try to find out whether the colour the client wishes to have is possible. By checking the client's hair you may see that it is in a bad condition and further treatment may not be appropriate.

Figure 8.5 Visually check hair to establish the condition

Tests

Carry out the following colour tests:

- skin test
- porosity test
- elasticity test
- incompatibility test
- strand/colour test
- test cutting.

Safety first

Always follow the manufacturer's instructions when testing. Record all results of tests carried out.

Contraindications

Any contraindications that you find will not allow you to carry out the colour service. These include:

- skin disorders
- damaged hair
- negative skin test
- sensitive scalp
- history of allergic reactions
- product incompatibility
- medical advice/instructions.

WWW Online activity 8.2

Correct selection

Colour correction problems

Problems you may have to correct include:

- removing artificial hair colour
- re-colouring hair after hair colour reduction
- removing bands of colour
- bleached hair re-colouration
- correction of highlights/lowlights.

Removing artificial hair colour

Reasons for clients to have their tint removed include:

- to lighten permanently coloured hair
- too many colouring products used on hair (build-up)
- to remove tone.

Definition

Artificial: To be man-made.

Tint is removed either using the method of reduction (using colour reducers) or using bleach. Colour reducers are used to remove permanent hair colour (tint) through reduction.

Figure 8.6 This client wishes to have colour removed due to build-up of products

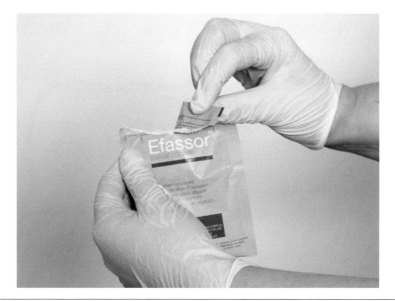

Figure 8.7 Colour reducer

Figure 8.8 Bleach

Oxidation and reduction

Oxidation is a chemical process involving the addition of oxygen to a substance. The hydrogen peroxide that is used in the colouring process contains the oxygen that allows oxidation to take place when colouring and bleaching hair.

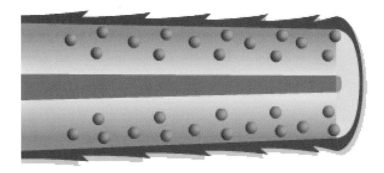

Figure 8.9 Colour molecules

The opposite of oxidation is reduction. Therefore it is the process of removing oxygen from a substance and adding hydrogen. The hydrogen forces the colour into smaller molecules so that they can be washed from the hair.

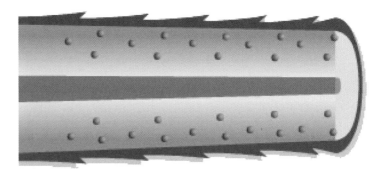

Figure 8.10 Hydrogen forces the colour into smaller molecules . . .

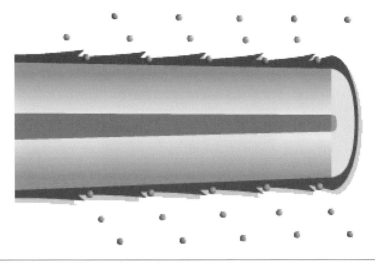

Figure 8.11 . . . so that they can be washed away

Re-colouring hair after hair colour reduction

Once the hair has had the colour removed, the target shade can be applied.

Figure 8.12 Hair that has had the colour removed

Bands of colour

Bands of colour are areas that appear darker or lighter than the rest of the hair. This is the result of either incorrect application of colour or colour fading. The application will depend on whether the bands of hair are lighter or darker than the rest of the hair. If the bands of colour are lighter, spot colouring can be a method to use for correcting this.

Figure 8.13 Bands of colour

Bleached hair re-colouration

If a client has bleached hair and wishes to re-colour, the first process is to carry out pre-pigmentation to add warmth, followed by the application of the target shade. As bleaching takes out the warm tones, which are red and yellow, these must be replaced before applying the target shade or else the hair will be a green colour.

> **Definition** 🔍
>
> **Pre-pigmentation:** Adding a warm colour to the hair before applying the target shade.

Figure 8.14 This client wishes to re-colour her bleached hair

Highlight or lowlight correction

If a client needs highlight or lowlight correction, it is usually due to the incorrect application of previous colour.

Figure 8.15 These highlights need correcting

8.3 Plan and agree a course of action to correct colour

Once you have determined the problem by obtaining all the information, you must decide on a course of action. You should have a good knowledge of the colouring products that are available in the salon so that you can recommend a suitable product and service based on your analysis of the client's colour problem.

Refer to Chapter 7 to refresh your knowledge on the products if necessary. Also refer to this unit for dealing with any problems that occur during the colouring process.

Present suitable options

When presenting the suitable options to the client, make sure you cover all possible methods with the products you will be using. Explain slowly, and make sure that the client understands fully the method and expected outcomes.

Figure 8.16 Present the suitable options to the client

Recommendations

As you have carried out a thorough analysis of the colour correction problem, you will have a recommendation. Explain carefully the reasons for your recommendation. If it is very unlikely that you will be able to achieve the client's wishes, then be truthful about this. For example, a negative skin test may not

Safety first ⚠️

A negative skin test may not allow a certain colour to be applied to the hair.

allow a certain colour to be applied to the hair. Explore all the other options with the client to achieve an outcome that the client is happy with. Make sure that your client is aware of the price and duration of the colour correction services.

Figure 8.17 Be truthful if you cannot carry out the service

Maintain the colour and future hairdressing services

Explain to your client how to maintain the colour that would result from the colour correction choice. The restrictions on any further hairdressing services should also be explained to the client. For example, once the colour has been reduced, and then re-coloured, the hair may be too weak to have certain chemical treatments applied.

Figure 8.18 Explain how to maintain the colour

Record the course of action

Once the client has made a decision based upon all the facts and recommendations you have made, you must record the course of action that you will be taking.

Online activity 8.4 | www

Round the board

8.4 Correct colour

This section will cover the methods of:

- removing artificial colour using colour reducers
- re-colouring hair that has had artificial colour removed
- removing bands of colour
- re-colouring bleached hair using pre-pigmentation and permanent colour
- correcting highlights and lowlights.

Preparing client's hair for colouring
Pre-colouring

If hair is very porous, the cuticles will be wide open and therefore will easily take in colour. However, it will not be able to keep the colour for very long and so is likely to fade quickly.

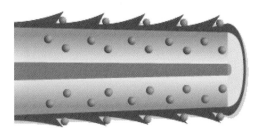

Figure 8.19 The cuticles are wide open and will easily take in colour

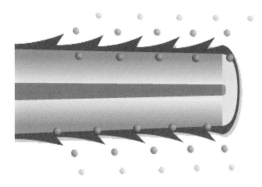

Figure 8.20 The colour particles will wash out quickly resulting in a faded colour

A pre-colouring treatment will help to improve the condition of hair by strengthening the internal structure, allowing the hair to keep in more of the colour particles.

Figure 8.21 Application of a pre-colouring treatment

Pre-softening

If hair is resistant to colour, it can be pre-softened. This lifts the cuticle to allow the colour to penetrate the cortex.

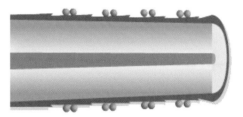

Figure 8.22 Colour molecules sitting on hair

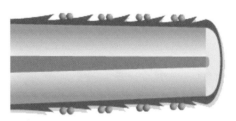

Figure 8.23 Pre-softening lifts the cuticle. . .

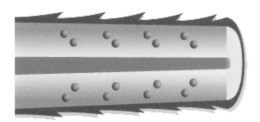

Figure 8.24 . . . which allows the colour to penetrate the cortex

Processing time and temperature

Processing time can be affected by temperature in the following ways:

- A warm salon will need less processing time than a cool salon.
- If the salon is cool extra heat can be applied but check the manufacturer's instructions first before applying.
- Natural heat from the scalp may affect the development time; therefore it may be necessary to apply products to mid-lengths and ends before roots.

Online activity 8.5 | **www**

correct

you

the

this

statements

choose

from

Can

?

list

Well Done!

Figure 8.25 Online activity screen

Correct selection

Preparing colour correction products

Before preparing and/or mixing colour correction products, always read the manufacturer's instructions carefully. Measure out products accurately, making sure you use the correct volume of hydrogen peroxide. Always wear the correct PPE.

> ⚠ **Safety first**
>
> Always read the manufacturer's instructions carefully when preparing colour correction products.

Figure 8.26 Take care when preparing colour correction products

Removing artificial colour using colour reducers

Figure 8.27 Before the service

Figure 8.28 The hair before colour reducer applied

Figure 8.29 Apply the colour reducer where the hair is darkest. Apply evenly but not to the regrowth area

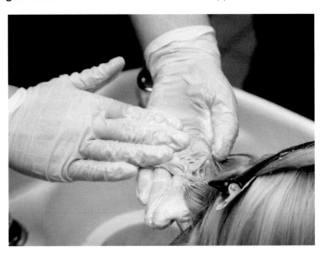

Figure 8.30 Use your hands to massage the product into the hair

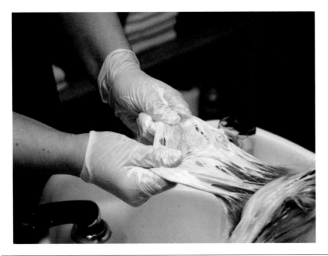

Figure 8.31 Development time will be affected by how porous the hair is, e.g. the areas where the hair is in worse condition will need less time than hair that is in good condition. Always stay with your client whilst the colour reducer is developing. This is because it might lighten more than expected

Figure 8.32 Rinse the hair with cool water to remove the colour reducer once the development time has been reached

Figure 8.33 Shampoo and rinse the hair

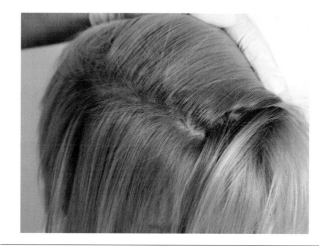

Figure 8.34 The hair colour once it has had the colour reducer applied. After the application of colour reducers, the client may be quite surprised at the result. Make sure the client is aware that this is not the end result

Re-colouring hair that has had artificial colour removed

Figure 8.35 Apply the chosen tint to the roots. Then apply to mid-lengths and ends

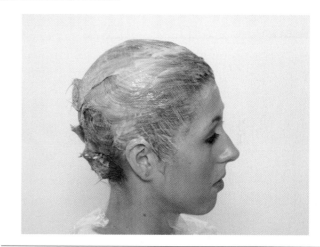

Figure 8.36 Leave for the recommended development time before rinsing off and styling

Figure 8.37 The target shade

WWW **Online activity 8.6**

Drag into correct order

Removing bands of colour

Figure 8.38 Bands of colour

Figure 8.39 Placing packets into the hair so that the colour does not smudge into the rest of the hair

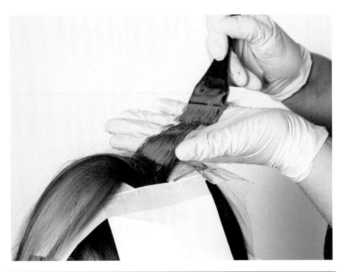

Figure 8.40 Applying tint directly to the lighter areas

Figure 8.41 The finished colour

Re-colouring bleached hair using pre-pigmentation and permanent colour

Figure 8.42 Semi-permanent or quasi-colour can be used for pre-pigmentation

Figure 8.43 After the client has been prepared in the appropriate manner, a warm shade is applied to the bleached hair

Figure 8.44 Leave to develop for the correct time. Rinse off the colour and shampoo

Figure 8.45 Hair after pre-pigmentation

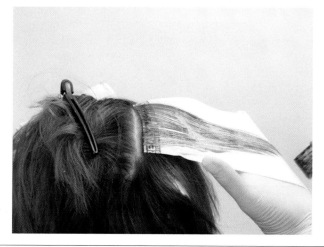

Figure 8.46 Apply permanent hair colour after pre-pigmentation. For the desired look, slices of a lighter colour are used to complement the full head of colour (online video). Leave to develop for the recommended time

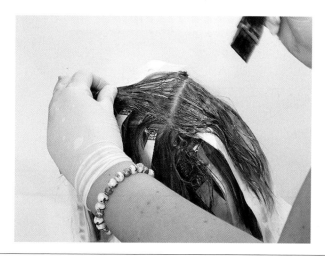

Figure 8.47 Applying target shade to the remaining hair

Figure 8.48 Rinse and shampoo the hair using suitable products

Figure 8.49 Finished look

Highlight and lowlight correction

Figure 8.50 Before the service

Figure 8.51 Section the hair in the appropriate way

Figure 8.52 Mix up three different strengths of bleach to correct the patchy highlights

Figure 8.53 Weave out sections of hair

Figure 8.54 Place the packet into the hair

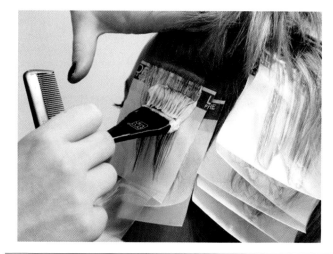

Figure 8.55 Apply the different strengths to hair as appropriate. The strongest peroxide is applied to the darkest areas and the weaker strength to the lighter. This will even out the colour

(Note: although not shown in this case, it is advisable to wear gloves whenever handling chemicals.)

Figure 8.56 Leave the hair to develop

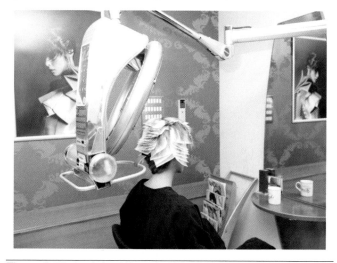

Figure 8.57 Apply heat if needed (check the manufacturer's instructions). Rinse off the colour and style as required

Figure 8.58 The finished look

www **Online activity 8.7**

Shoot the target

8.5 Provide aftercare advice

Throughout the colouring service, advise the client on the best products to use to maintain colour and condition. Also explain to the client what they should avoid as there are many products that can cause the colour to fade. The products that you recommend should also be based on the factors that influence the service including career and lifestyle.

Refer to Chapter 4 for information on promoting products and services.

Time between appointments

You should explain to the client how often they should return to the salon to maintain their colour. This will depend on the type of colour. For example, a client who has had a full head colour should be advised to return to the salon after 4–5 weeks to have their regrowth coloured whereas those with highlights/lowlights could return after 2–4 months.

The time between appointments will also depend on the client's wishes. Most clients will want to have their hair re-coloured once they start seeing regrowth.

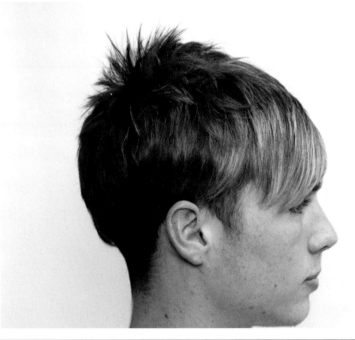

Figure 8.59 Recommended times between appointments will depend on the style

Safety first

Give clients health and safety advice about electrical equipment.

Electrical equipment

When explaining to the client the use of heated styling equipment, take care giving health and safety advice. Continual use will damage the hair. Therefore regular conditioning and using heat protectors are advisable.

8.6 Worksheets

WORKSHEETS

You can carry out the worksheets during your study of a chapter or unit, or at the end. An example is presented here and there are more online. If your college or company is registered with ATT Training, lots more are available. Write your answers directly in the book, but only if you own it of course – if it is a library or college book, use a separate piece of paper!

8.6.1 Removing artificial colour using colour reducers

Answer the following questions:

1. Which tests should be carried out prior to colour removal?

2. What must you always do when mixing up colour reducers?

3. Where should you apply the colour reducer first?

4. Where must you avoid applying the colour reducer?

5. Which factors will affect development time?

6. Why should you always stay with your client whilst the colour reducer is developing?

7. What temperature of water should you use to remove the colour reducer?

8. Which products should be used on the hair at this stage?

8.7 Assessment

Well done! If you have studied all the content of this unit you may be ready to test your knowledge.

Check out the 'Preparing for assessments' section in Chapter 1 if you have not already done so, and always remember:

- You can only do your best if you have. . .
  - studied hard
  - completed the activities
  - completed the worksheets
  - practised, practised, practised
  - and then revised!

? Now carry out the online multiple-choice quiz

. . . and good luck in the final exam, which will be arranged by your tutor/assessor.

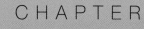

Style and dress hair

This chapter covers the NVQ/SVQ unit GH19, Creatively syle and dress hair; and VRQ unit 305, Style and dress hair to create a variety of looks.

This chapter will cover different styling and dressing techniques to be carried out in a creative and innovative way. The importance of using your imagination to create styles cannot be overemphasised. The techniques and effects that will be covered include added hair, setting (pin curling and finger waving),

blow-drying and the use of heated styling equipment.

In this chapter you will learn about:

- maintaining effective and safe methods of working when styling hair

- styling and dressing hair creatively

- providing aftercare advice.

CHAPTER 9 STYLE AND DRESS HAIR: CONTENTS, SCREENS AND ACTIVITIES

Key:

Sections from the book are set in this colour

Screens available online are set in this colour

Online activity screens are set in this colour

Working safely

Introduction	Mousses
Preparing client for styling	Hair serums
Comfort during styling	Setting lotion
Styling tools and equipment	Gels
Correct selection	Heat protectors
Hair is hygroscopic	Hairsprays
Styling products	Creams
Round the board	Wax
	Five in a row

Creatively style and dress hair

Introduction	Creating a zigzag look using unconventional items 2
Consultation	
Round the board	Creating a zigzag look using unconventional items 3
The occasion	
Recommendations	Creating a zigzag look using unconventional items 4
Techniques of styling and effects	
Added hair	Creating a zigzag look using unconventional items 5
Check it	
Setting	Creating a look using unconventional items 1
Pin curling	
Finger waving	Creating a look using unconventional items 2
Winding techniques	
Blow-drying	Creating a look using unconventional items 3
Heated styling equipment – heated tongs	
	Creating a look using unconventional items 4
Hair straighteners	
Round the board	Scrambled words
Creating a zigzag look using unconventional items 1	Styling incorporating finger waves and pin curls
	Checking balance of completed style

Provide aftercare advice

Introduction	Removal of hairstyle
Products	Worksheet – Recommendations
	Online multiple choice quiz

9.1 Working safely

When styling and dressing hair, you will use many different products, tools and equipment. This section covers health and safety requirements necessary for their use. Chapter 2 covers more general health and safety working methods in more detail. Refer to this unit if necessary.

Preparing client for styling

Assist the client to put on a suitably sized gown to protect their clothing whilst in the salon. After the hair is shampooed, it is combed through to untangle.

Figure 9.1 Client is ready for styling

Comfort during styling

Whilst styling and finishing the client's hair, it is important for you to move around the client's head. However, the client's comfort should be considered at all times. Their back should be positioned right to the back of the chair and as flat as possible. They should have both feet on the footrest or the floor. Not only will this be a more comfortable position for the client but it also enables you to create a balanced hairstyle. Your own comfort during styling and finishing should be considered as well. Check your posture is correct, ensuring that your client's seat is at the correct height for you to work. Ensure that your work area is tidy and free from clutter.

Definition

Posture: The position of a person's body when sitting or standing.

Styling equipment and tools

Tools and equipment used for styling and dressing the hair include:

- brushes and combs
- hand dryers and attachments

- rollers and pins
- heated styling equipment including rollers, straighteners, crimping irons and tongs
- unconventional items including chopsticks, rags, straws, clothes hangers, foam rods, pots wrapped in foil, ends of other equipment, e.g. pin-tail comb.

As with conventional items, always consider the health and safety implications when working with unconventional items. These include:

- Is the item sterile and clean, and if not, can it be sterilised and cleaned?
- Is the item safe under all circumstances?
- Is the item fit for the purpose it is to be used for?

Ensure that all equipment is ready before you use it.

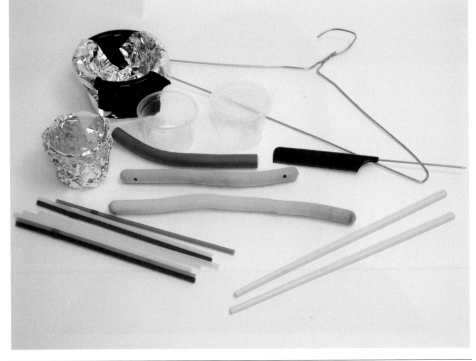

Figure 9.2 A selection of unconventional items that can be used when styling and dressing hair

WWW **Online activity 9.1**

Correct selection

Hair is hygroscopic

This means that it has the ability to absorb moisture.

Wet hair can be stretched nearly double its normal length. This is called elasticity. Wet hair in its stretched state is called the 'beta keratin'. When it is in the natural state (unstretched), the hair is called the 'alpha keratin'. The reason why hair stretches is that the hydrogen bonds are broken down by water. It is these properties that allow us to alter the shape of hair. When heat is applied the hydrogen bonds can be re-formed into a new shape. The humidity in the air will affect the structure of the hair by making the hair feel damp. This will take the hair back to its natural state.

View the online video to learn more about the hair in its various states.

Styling products

Figure 9.3 A selection of products

These include:

- mousses
- serums
- creams
- setting lotions
- gels
- heat protectors
- sprays
- creams
- waxes.

To prevent wastage of products, only use the amount needed according to manufacturers' instructions.

Online activity 9.2

Round the board

Mousses

Mousses are available in different strengths. They are applied to wet hair with the hands and will hold style in place and achieve a soft effect.

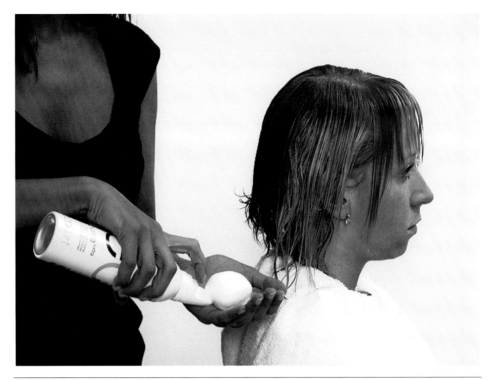

Figure 9.4 Mousse is applied to wet hair

Hair serums

Hair serum will make hair look shiny and in better condition. This product must be used sparingly as it is very concentrated and can make hair appear lank or greasy.

Figure 9.5 Use serum sparingly

Setting lotion

Setting lotion is applied sparingly onto wet hair to ensure an even application, and massaged into the hair. This helps hold the set in place and acts as a film to protect from weather and humidity. It gives lots of body to fine or limp hair.

> **Definition**
>
> **Humidity:** Moisture in the air.

Figure 9.6 Applying setting lotion

Gels

Gels are designed to be used on either wet or dry hair. They complement and give definition to the style.

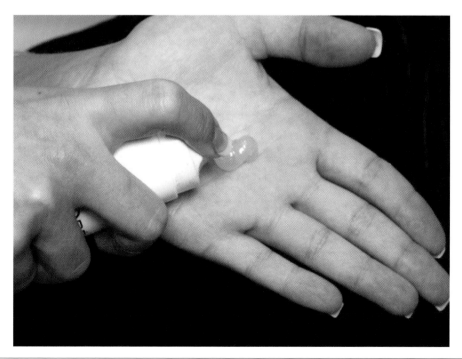

Figure 9.7 Applying gel

Heat protectors

These products protect the hair from damage caused by using heated styling equipment. When heated styling equipment is used frequently, the hair structure can become damaged as the cuticle swells and rises. When heat applicators are applied, they form a shield around the hair which acts as a barrier and absorbs the heat.

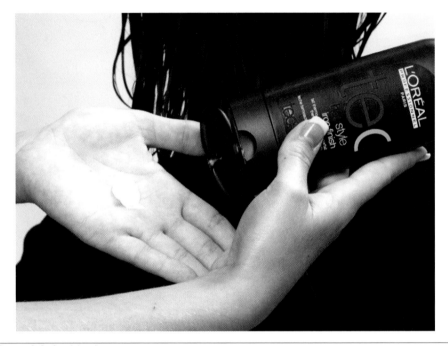

Figure 9.8 Applying heat protector

Hairsprays

Hairspray holds the hair in place and protects the hair from the weather and humidity. It comes in different strengths and it is easily removed from the hair by brushing or wetting as most hairsprays are water soluble.

Safety first

When using hairspray, always point the spray away from the client's face.

Figure 9.9 Application of hairspray

Creams

Creams can be used on wet or dry hair and should be used sparingly. They are used to give moisture and curl definition to the hair.

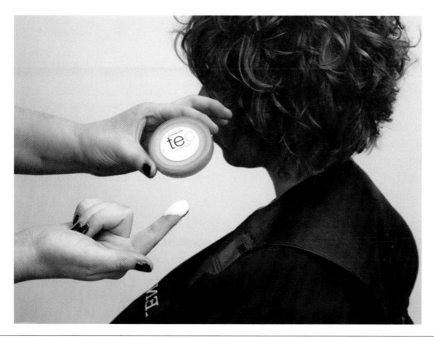

Figure 9.10 Applying cream

Wax

Wax is used on dry hair to separate curls and give definition to the hair.

Figure 9.11 Applying wax

Online activity 9.3 WWW

Five in a row

9.2 Creatively style and dress hair

In this section you will be developing different creative styling and dressing techniques and effects whilst considering the client's hair structure, face shape and other influencing factors.

Consultation

Definitions

Interpreted: To make sense of.

Accurate: Exact.

Before any service begins the hairdresser must find out what the client wants or needs. The consultation is used to ensure the client's wishes are interpreted accurately and the desired look achieved. It is essential to be factual, honest, tactful, sincere, direct and clear. Take a look at what the client is wearing to determine their current style. This will help when deciding on the final look. Visual aids can help to communicate with the client. They may bring in a picture of a particular style they wish to have.

Figure 9.12 Visual aids can help you to communicate

WWW **Online activity 9.4**

Round the board

The occasion

Most of the time, a client who has their hair styled and dressed will want it for a special occasion. These occasions include:

* weddings
* parties
* proms/balls.

Make sure you find out the occasion and match the look to this. For example, a formal occasion would suit a classic or current look. Ask the client what outfit they will be wearing and match accordingly.

If the hair is to be styled for a wedding, make sure that you ask the bride to collect many different visual aids of the look that she wishes to achieve. Ask her to bring in a picture of the dress that she will be wearing and examples of the theme for her forthcoming wedding. This helps you to form a clear picture of the look that she wishes to have.

Figure 9.13 A style suitable for an occasion

Figure 9.14 Visual aids will help when picking a style for an occasion

Recommendations

Maintain high standards of care during the consultation as this will ensure happy clients and reflect well on your salon's image. The influencing factors upon which your recommendations will be based include:

- head and face shape
- growth patterns
- hair texture
- haircut
- hair length
- hair density
- hair elasticity.

Once these factors have been taken into consideration and you have made your recommendations make sure the client is happy with the style before starting the service.

Key information

Refer to Chapter 3 for more information about influencing factors.

Figure 9.15 Checking the hair

Techniques of styling and effects

This Level 3 styling unit involves using a combination of techniques to create different effects. Be creative and original in your choice of technique.

The main techniques and effects of styling are:

- added hair
- setting, including pin curling and finger waving
- blow-drying
- use of heated styling equipment.

Key information

You should be creative and original in your choice of styling technique.

Added hair

The popularity of added hair changes frequently. There are many different types and it can have the following main effects when styled into a client's hair:

- adds length
- adds colour
- adds volume.

Using added hair gives you the opportunity to carry out many more creative styles so do not dismiss the opportunity if it arises. Make sure the added hair blends well into the style and do not allow the base to be seen. It should be secured so that it does not pull on the roots of the hair. This applies to other hair accessories as well.

Figure 9.16 Added hair

Figure 9.17 Securing added hair

Figure 9.18 Added hair incorporated into style

Online activity 9.5 **www**

Check it

Setting

Setting involves placing the hair into chosen positions and keeping it there whilst it forms a shape. This may be achieved by using many different techniques including pin curling and finger waving. Setting hair can create movement within the hair and decrease or increase volume.

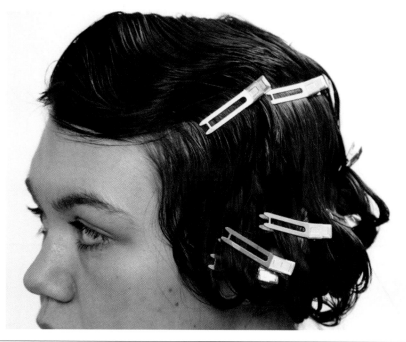

Figure 9.19 Setting can be achieved through pin curling and finger waving

Pin curling

There are three main types of pin curling effects:

- Barrel curls sit off base to give volume and lift to the hair.
- Open-centred pin curls are loose, soft pin curls which sit off base and are usually used in the nape or the sides of the head where a loose, flattering effect needs to be achieved.
- Clock-spring pin curls are used to create very tight curls or wave movements.

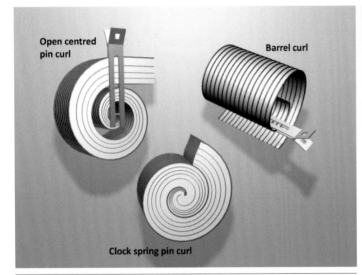

Figure 9.20 The three main types of pin curl

Figure 9.21 Barrel curls (with cotton wool) and open centred pin curls

Finger waving

Finger waving is often referred to as 'water waving'. It was popular with early movie stars. The technique involves moulding hair into the shape of the letter 'S' with fingers and a comb. The technique was popular before rollers and pin curls. It has a very flat effect on the head.

Figure 9.22 Finger waving 1

Figure 9.23 Finger waving 2

Figure 9.24 Finger waving 3

Winding techniques

You will be using a variety of winding techniques to create a number of effects. The hair can be wound using a 'point to root' or 'root to point' method. Both winding techniques can be carried out using unconventional items.

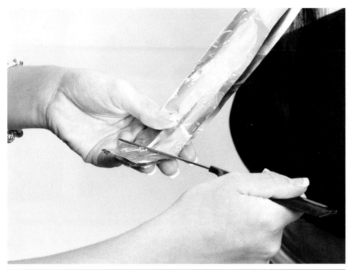

Figure 9.25 Point to root winding

Figure 9.26 Root to point winding

Blow-drying

Blow-drying techniques include:

* finger drying
* scrunch drying
* using hairdryer with different size brushes.

Figure 9.27 Finger drying

Figure 9.28 Scrunch drying

Heated styling equipment – heated tongs

To give a conventional curl, use a point to root technique. To achieve a spiral look, wind the hair around the tongs using a root to point technique.

Figure 9.29 Point to root (online video)

Figure 9.30 Root to point (online video)

Hair straighteners

When carrying out creative styles, straighteners can be used to either straighten or curl the hair in many different fashions.

Figure 9.31 Straighteners can be used to curl . . .

Figure 9.32 . . . and style in different fashions

WWW **Online activity 9.6**

Round the board

Creating a zigzag look using unconventional items

Figure 9.33 Prepare the hair for this look by sectioning dry hair

Figure 9.34 Strips of foil are placed into the hair starting from the roots to the ends. They are then folded over in half. The foil is secured to the root area using a clip

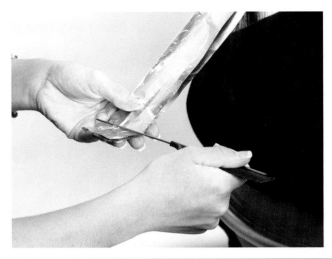

Figure 9.35 Starting at the bottom of the foil, fold over approximately 5 cm

Figure 9.36 Then fold the same amount in the reverse direction

Figure 9.37 Fold in the reverse direction again . . .

Figure 9.38 . . . working up to. . .

Figure 9.39 . . . the roots of the hair. Using the clip that is holding the hair, secure the folded up packet

Figure 9.40 This method creates a zigzag effect

Figure 9.41 Continue throughout the head in the same way

Figure 9.42 Using heated straighteners, press each packet for approximately half a minute. Be methodical, start at the nape area and heat every packet

Figure 9.43 Remove each packet by starting at the nape. This will allow the hair to cool down

Figure 9.44 The hair after all the packets are removed

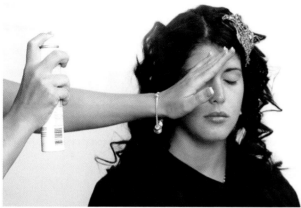

Figure 9.45 Dress out the style with your fingers. Apply finishing products and accessories as appropriate

Figure 9.46 The finished look

Creating a look using unconventional items

Figure 9.47 Take small sections of hair and apply product

Figure 9.48 Twist the pieces of hair around the end of a pin-tail comb. Only twist the mid-lengths of the hair; leave the roots and ends. Use the hair straighteners to set the curl

Figure 9.49 Carry on this process all around the head until the whole head of hair has had this curling technique applied

Figure 9.50 The hair after the curling process is completed

Figure 9.51 Brush out the curls to loosen the hair and create a full effect

Figure 9.52 The hair once the curls have been brushed out

Figure 9.53 Tie the hair up into the style using hairgrips. Ensure that none of the grips can be seen

Figure 9.54 The finished style

WWW **Online activity 9.7**

Scrambled words

Style incorporating finger waves and pin curls

Figure 9.55 Apply appropriate moulding product to the hair to help create finger waves

Figure 9.56 Finger wave the front hairline

Figure 9.57 A variety of pin curls have been . . .

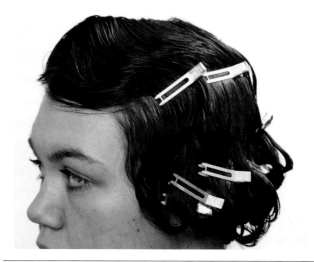

Figure 9.58 . . . used over the remainder of the head

Figure 9.59 Dress the hair and use appropriate finishing products

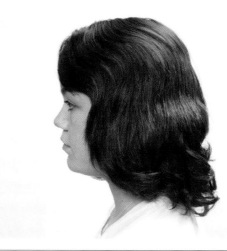

Figure 9.60 The finished style

Checking balance of completed style

Check the balance of the hairstyle, using the front mirror to ensure that the profile shape of the hairstyle and the finish appeal to the client. Reinforce this by confirming it with the client. Use a back mirror from behind, angling the position so both you and the client can see the finished result from the back.

Definition

Reinforce: To make information sink in. To confirm.

Figure 9.61 Checking balance of hairstyle

9.3 Provide aftercare advice

An important part of this service is to give the client aftercare advice. Ensure the client is aware that if the hair becomes damp through weather conditions, it is likely to drop or revert back to its natural state. Throughout the service you must explain to the client what you are doing. Do this fully and accurately, repeating yourself if necessary.

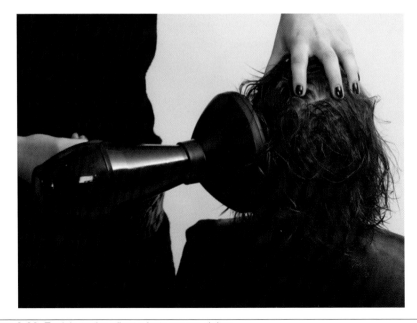

Figure 9.62 Explain to the client what you are doing

Products

Advise the client which products can be used at home. This should be based on the factors that influence the service. Refer to Chapter 4 for more information.

Removal of hairstyle

Explain to the client the way in which the hairstyle is taken down. Pins and grips must be removed carefully before brushing the hair. Suggest to your client that if the hair has been backcombed, they should brush the hair gently starting at the ends of the hair and going towards the roots. The client should be advised to have added hair removed at the salon. All accessories should be removed carefully without pulling the hair.

Figure 9.63 Added hair should be removed at the salon

WORKSHEETS

9.4 Worksheets

You can carry out the worksheets during your study of a chapter or unit, or at the end. An example is presented here and there are more online. If your college or company is registered with ATT Training, lots more are available. Write your answers directly in the book, but only if you own it of course – if it is a library or college book, use a separate piece of paper!

9.4.1 Recommendations

Maintain high standards of care during the consultation as this will ensure happy clients and reflect well on your salon's image. There are a number of influencing factors that should be taken into consideration. When you have made your recommendations make sure the client is happy with the style decision before starting the service.

What are the influencing factors that you should consider when making recommendations to clients?

1. _____

2. _____

3. _____

4. _____

5. _____

6. _____

7. _____

9.5 Assessment

Well done! If you have studied all the content of this unit you may be ready to test your knowledge.

Check out the 'Preparing for assessments' section in Chapter 1 if you have not already done so, and always remember:

- You can only do your best if you have. . .
  - studied hard
  - completed the activities
  - completed the worksheets
  - practised, practised, practised
  - and then revised!

Now carry out the online multiple-choice quiz **?**

. . . and good luck in the final exam, which will be arranged by your tutor/assessor.

10.4 Worksheets

WORKSHEETS

You can carry out the worksheets during your study of a chapter or unit, or at the end. An example is presented here and there are more online. If your college or company is registered with ATT Training, lots more are available. Write your answers directly in the book, but only if you own it of course – if it is a library or college book, use a separate piece of paper!

10.4.1 Plaits, rolls, knots and twists

Describe each of the four images below, giving as much detail as possible. Include the name of the style and a description of how to achieve it.

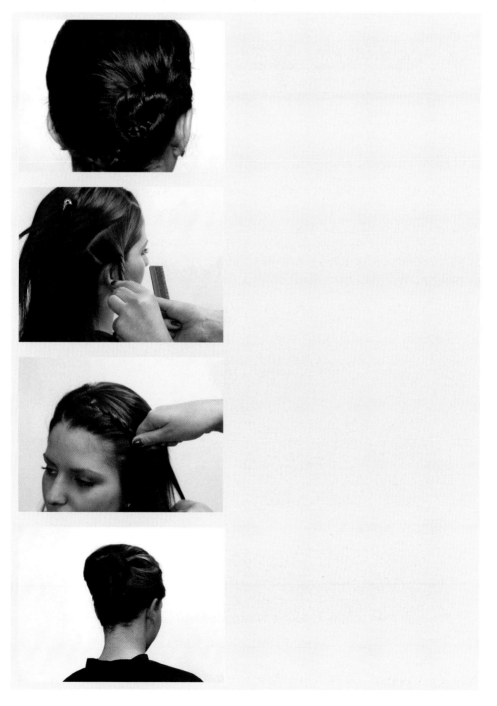

10.5 Assessment

Well done! If you have studied all the content of this unit you may be ready to test your knowledge.

Check out the 'Preparing for assessments' section in Chapter 1 if you have not already done so, and always remember:

- You can only do your best if you have. . .
  - ○ studied hard
  - ○ completed the activities
  - ○ completed the worksheets
  - ○ practised, practised, practised
  - ○ and then revised!

? Now carry out the online multiple-choice quiz

. . . and good luck in the final exam, which will be arranged by your tutor/assessor.

Develop creative skills

This chapter covers the NVQ/SVQ unit GH21, Develop and enhance your creative hairdressing skills; and VRQ unit 316, Creative hairdressing design skills.

This chapter covers the skills needed to enhance your creativity. This involves not only creating a variety of techniques used in hairdressing but also the planning and designing that must be carried out before and the evaluation after. Team working is of key importance for this area of hairdressing.

In this chapter you will learn about:

- planning and designing a range of images
- producing a range of creative images
- evaluating your results against the design plan objectives.

CHAPTER 11 DEVELOP CREATIVE SKILLS: CONTENTS, SCREENS AND ACTIVITIES

Key:

Sections from the book are set in this colour

Screens available online are set in this colour

Online activity screens are set in this colour

Plan and design a range of images

Introduction	Budgeting
Researching your ideas	Outgoings
Basic principles of design, scale and proportion	Venue requirements
	Correct selection
Round the board	Resources
Image elements	Health and safety
Design planning	Likely hazards and risks
Objectives	Problem solving
Roles and responsibilities	Shoot the target
Five in a row	Agreeing your design plan

Produce a range of creative images

Introduction	Additional media
Techniques used	Finished look
Changing circumstances	Round the board

Evaluate your results against the design plan objectives

Introduction	Methods of feedback
Feedback from others	Worksheet – Budgeting
Judging yourself	Online multiple choice quiz
Scrambled words	

11.1 Plan and design a range of images

Before creating your images you must make sure that you are aware of the activity for which you are working. These activities include:

- competitions
- shows
- photographic work.

Your choice will be influenced by how experienced you are and the amount of financial support you receive with your salon backing you.

Figure 11.1 You will be assessed by judges in competition work

Figure 11.2 Shows

Figure 11.3 Photographic work

Researching your ideas

You may need to research your theme. This is especially relevant if your theme is historical or cultural. To research your theme you can use the following sources of information:

- television
- Internet
- magazines
- trade journals.

Figure 11.4 Magazines and trade journals

Basic principles of design, scale and proportion

You should consider the basic principles of design, scale and proportion when creating your image. It is important to check the balance; it will be either symmetrical or asymmetrical. Make sure that your image has the correct scale and proportion to complement the desired look. For example, a simple hairstyle may be lost on a model who wears a large flamboyant outfit.

Definition

Flamboyant: To be excessively ornamented.

Figure 11.5 Make sure the image has the correct scale and proportion

Online activity 11.1 **WWW**

Round the board

Image elements

Hairdressing creativity involves using elements to create a whole image. This not only relates to the hair but also to the make-up and clothes. Some of these components are:

- using angles and lines to establish the visual effect
- shape and form to mentally interpret the image
- colours used for the image (depth and tone)
- texture of the components in the image
- techniques used to create the style.

Figure 11.6 Hairdressing creativity involves using elements to create a whole image

Figure 11.7 Make-up and clothes are an important consideration when creating an image

Definitions

Comprehensive: To cover a wide area.

Objectives: The goals to be achieved.

Design plan: A document used for planning a project outlining objectives, budget, roles and responsibilities, resources, health and safety issues, etc.

Design planning

Your design plan should be comprehensive and should define the following:

- objectives
- roles and responsibilities
- budget
- venue requirements
- resources
- health and safety
- potential problems and how to resolve them.

Objectives

Your design plan must include your objectives. These are simply what you wish to achieve. These objectives may be to increase your:

- customer base
- revenue
- profile
- job satisfaction
- training of staff.

Make sure your objectives are clearly stated and measured in some context so that after the activity you can establish whether your objectives have been met. Your design plan will be covering images based on a theme, or avant-garde.

Roles and responsibilities

Clearly define the roles and responsibilities of those involved. You will be using your communication skills to do this. Ensure that other members of the team have understood what you have said by asking them to repeat what you have asked them to do. Again this means that if you have been asked to perform a task, you should clarify your instructions.

Meetings should be regular, either formal or informal. Any queries can be raised at this time. Encourage all members to talk by creating breaks in the conversation. Listen to other team members for their tone of voice or body language. They may be showing signs that they are struggling with some concepts. If this is the case then offer your support in a way that is appropriate.

When a decision has been made over one focal point, move on to the next. Summarise at the end of the meeting so everybody is clear about their role and responsibility for the activity.

Definition

Avant-garde: A term used to describe artwork that breaks away from tradition.

Key information

Make sure your objectives are clearly stated and measured in some context so that after the activity you can establish whether your objectives have been met.

Figure 11.8 Encourage all team members to participate in meetings

www   Online activity 11.2

Five in a row

Budgeting

Financial planning is essential when working on an activity. Once the budget is set, you must keep to it. The money that is made from carrying out the activity must be more than what is spent. When creating a budget, you must be realistic. There is little point in just making up figures; if your budget is exceeded, your objectives will not be met. Make sure you think of everything that you will need to buy for the activity, however small. If budgeting for a hair show or demonstration, an option would be to set a price for the tickets in order to cover some if not all of your outgoings.

Key information

Stick to your budget – the money that is made from carrying out the activity must be more than what is spent!

Figure 11.9 Creating a budget on the computer

Outgoings

Your budget may include payments for the following:

- models
- special guest
- judges
- photographer
- clothes
- make-up
- venue
- lighting and sound
- equipment
- transport
- food
- drink
- staff
- marketing.

Figure 11.10 You may need a make-up artist

Venue requirements

Decide where the event will be held. Venues could be:

- your salon
- hotel
- hall.

Figure 11.11 Activities may be held in a salon

Figure 11.12 Activities may be held in a hall

Make sure that the following is considered before booking a venue:

- Will there be the right number of plug sockets to use and will they be in the right area?
- Will the venue be able to cope with the power surge?
- Will lighting and sound be provided by the venue?
- Will there be basins available to shampoo models' hair?
- Is there an area where the models can dress?
- If supplying food and drink, does the venue have the correct licence?
- Is it possible to set up a stage for hair shows/demonstrations at the venue if necessary?

Make sure you have enough time before the activity to set it up. Ensure that this is possible with the chosen venue.

Figure 11.13 Ensure you consider lighting and stage if needed

Online activity 11.3 **www**

Correct selection

Resources

The design plan should include all details about your resources that you will need for the activity. Products to be used should be listed, as should any props that are required. Extra consideration may be needed for additional media, e.g. any clothes or accessories used. This is because you may have to hire these, for a fee. Sometimes retailers will allow you to use their items for publicity. This will reduce your outgoings significantly. Other resources include the number of staff that will be attending the activity.

Figure 11.14 Ensure that you know the number of staff required for the activity and include this information in your design plan

Health and safety

Ensure that you adhere to all health and safety regulations when carrying out any kind of activity. Keep in mind at all times the following legislation:

* Health and Safety at Work etc. Act
* Electricity at Work Regulations
* COSHH
* Personal Protective Equipment Regulations
* Manual Handling Operations Regulations.

Ensure that you are aware of the venue's own health and safety procedures.

Safety first

Ensure that you adhere to all health and safety regulations when carrying out any kind of activity.

Figure 11.15 Take care when using electrical equipment

Figure 11.16 Read the manufacturer's instructions before using chemicals

Likely hazards and risks

When working at a different venue, you must be aware of the hazards. A hazard is a source of danger. Examples of hazards include the following:

- electrical equipment
- products
- trailing leads.

It may be that you will have to carry out a risk assessment for the activity. The risk is the likelihood of an accident occurring from the hazard.

Definition 🔍

Risk assessment: The process of calculating the risk associated with a hazard and the actions taken to avoid it.

Figure 11.17 Electrical equipment

Figure 11.18 Products

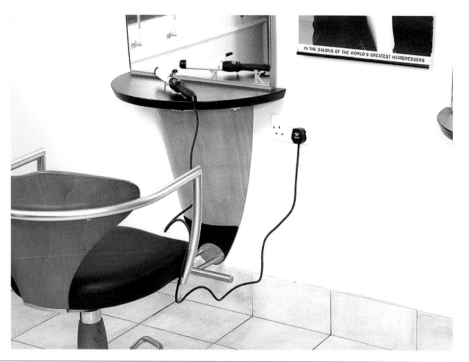

Figure 11.19 Trailing leads

Problem solving

Make sure you know what to do if a problem arises during the event. Problems are likely to occur at these kinds of occasions, so be prepared for problems and if they do occur, act efficiently and without panicking.

Tables 11.1, 11.2 and 11.3 show some of the problems that may occur at photographic shoots, hair shows and competitions. The tables also show ways of resolving problems. You will notice that most problems are avoided by making sure you have planned for every eventuality.

Table 11.1 Problems that may occur at photographic shoots

Problem	Resolved by:
Model does not turn up	Ensure there are stand-ins
Equipment does not work	Carry spares
Film runs out	Carry spares

Table 11.2 Problems that may occur at hair shows

Problem	Resolved by:
Model does not turn up	Ensure there are stand-ins
Model turns up late	Always allow extra time
Equipment does not work	Carry spares
Show overruns	Ensure venue will allow extra time
Gaps in performance	Fill with music
Problems with lighting/sound	Check everything works beforehand

Table 11.3 Problems that may occur with competition work

Problem	Resolved by:
Model does not turn up	Ensure there are stand-ins
Equipment does not work	Carry spares
Competition rules broken	Make sure that any rules are read beforehand
Not taken the right equipment	Ask others for help
Time runs out	Practise beforehand

WWW **Online activity 11.4**

Shoot the target

Agreeing your design plan

Once you are happy with your design plan and you have included everything needed, it is time for you to show this to the appropriate person or persons. This/ these could be your colleagues, line manager, make-up artists, photographer, competition judges or show audience.

Figure 11.20 Agreeing design plan with line manager

Present your design plan using excellent communication skills. You may need to present an argument for showing a style you feel strongly about when you know that the person you are presenting it to does not agree. If they still do not agree with you after you have used a varied vocabulary to present your case, you should think very carefully about this. Do not lose your temper, and decide whether they have a fair point. Once any modifications have been made, you can create your image/s.

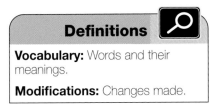

Definitions

Vocabulary: Words and their meanings.

Modifications: Changes made.

Figure 11.21 Use excellent communication skills to present your case

11.2 Produce a range of creative images

Once all your planning has been carried out, it is time to implement the design plan. Whilst doing this, make sure that you work well with others involved and use excellent communication and interpersonal skills. Maintain strict confidentiality about issues concerning the activity you are working on. If you do not do this at all times, other salons may hear of your ideas thus preventing the surprise on the day. Others may also plagiarise your ideas. Acting in the appropriate way will promote good working relationships for the future.

 **Definitions**

Interpersonal skills: The ability to deal well with different people.

Confidentiality: To keep secret.

Plagiarise: Taking another person's work as your own.

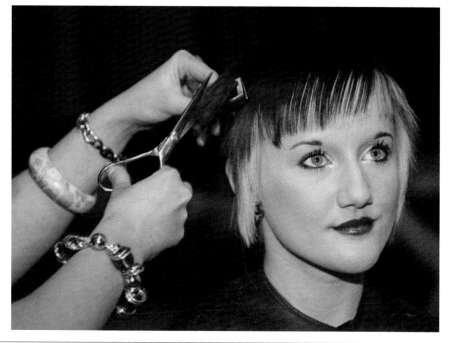

Figure 11.22 Implementing the design plan

Techniques used

When creating your image, you may be using any of the following techniques:

- cutting
- colouring
- perming
- relaxing
- added hair
- plaiting
- twisting
- shaving
- patterns in hair
- locking
- styling and dressing.

Refer to Chapters 9 and 10 for more information on the products and techniques used during styling and dressing, including added hair. You should follow safe working methods throughout.

Changing circumstances

In case circumstances change when you are producing you creative images, you must make sure that your plan is adaptable. For example, you may not be able to use the same model for some reason. If this is the case expand your design plan to suit your new model.

Figure 11.23 Ensure that your plan is adapatable

Additional media

Make sure that your chosen additional media (e.g. make-up, clothes and accessories) complement the look. If you are having photographs taken, keep in mind that magazines usually work 3 months ahead. This means the outfits,

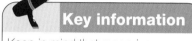

make-up and accessories should reflect this time and not the current time. Keep everything neutral if you do not wish the photographs to date.

Figure 11.24 Ensure that additional media complement the look

Key information

Keep in mind that magazines usually work 3 months ahead so you should ensure that the outfits, make-up and accessories reflect this.

Finished look

Once you have finished, check your design plan and make sure you are happy with the finished look you have created. Check that it enhances your profile by showing off your innovative abilities.

Definition

Innovative: To be forward thinking in terms of ideas and themes.

Figure 11.25 Online activity screen

Round the board

11.3 Evaluate your results against the design plan objectives

During and after the activity you should ask for feedback from the other people involved. This enables you to evaluate the effectiveness of your design plan and what you hoped to achieve from your image. It is the best way of improving your work and will help you to evaluate how you can adapt your design plan for commercial work. For example, the image could be used for photographic displays. Carry out your evaluation as soon after the activity as possible as you will remember everything best at this time.

Feedback from others

The following people can give you feedback:

- colleagues
- line manager
- models
- make-up artists
- audience
- photographer
- competition judges.

Do not take offence when these people give you feedback. Remember that it should all be constructive criticism.

Figure 11.26 You can ask your line manager to give you feedback

Figure 11.27 You can also ask the judges for feedback

Judging yourself

You can also give yourself feedback by looking at your image critically and deciding which parts could do with some improvement. Decide whether you have met the objectives that you set in your design plan.

www   **Online activity 11.6**

Scrambled words

Methods of feedback

This will mostly be done verbally but you may also hand out questionnaires to the audience for example. During hairdressing shows you may also pick up ways of assessing how the audience feels about your work. Look at their body language. Do they look relaxed or are they fidgeting? A relaxed audience suggests they are interested in the show and therefore your work is appreciated.

Figure 11.28 Look at the audience's body language to see how interested they are

Key information

A relaxed audience suggests they are interested in the show and therefore your work is appreciated.

11

11.4 Worksheets

You can carry out the worksheets during your study of a chapter or unit, or at the end. An example is presented here and there are more online. If your college or company is registered with ATT Training, lots more are available. Write your answers directly in the book, but only if you own it of course – if it is a library or college book, use a separate piece of paper!

11.4.1 Budgeting

Financial planning is essential when working on an activity. Once the budget is set, you must keep to it.

Try this exercise to get an idea of budgeting:

> Your objective is to get at least 1 new image for your portfolio. You need to find a model and create at least 1 new hairstyle to be photographed. Your salon allows you to use their facilities and products, but you must provide everything else. You have a budget of £100.

Here is a table to get you started:

Activity	Cost	Total amount left to spend
Buy magazines for inspiration	£5	£95

11.5 Assessment

Well done! If you have studied all the content of this unit you may be ready to test your knowledge.

Check out the 'Preparing for assessments' section in Chapter 1 if you have not already done so, and always remember:

- You can only do your best if you have. . .
  - studied hard
  - completed the activities
  - completed the worksheets
  - practised, practised, practised
  - and then revised!

Now carry out the online multiple-choice quiz **?**

. . . and good luck in the final exam, which will be arranged by your tutor/assessor.

Design and create facial hair shapes

This chapter covers the NVQ/SVQ unit GB7, *Design and create facial hair shapes.*

The cutting techniques learnt previously are an essential part of cutting beards and moustaches. This chapter looks at the different designs that can be created using the scissor over comb, clipper over comb and freehand techniques.

In this chapter you will learn about:

- maintaining effective and safe methods of working when cutting facial hair
- creating a range of facial hair shapes
- providing aftercare advice.

CHAPTER 12 DESIGN AND CREATE FACIAL HAIR SHAPES: CONTENTS, SCREENS AND ACTIVITIES

Key:
Sections from the book are set in this colour
Screens available online are set in this colour
Online activity screens are set in this colour

Working safely

Introduction
Preparing the client for facial cutting
Comfort during cutting facial hair
Keep work area tidy
Tools and equipment
Scissors
Round the board
Combs
Clippers
Clipper attachments
Towels and gowns

Correct selection
Consultation
Factors influencing the service
Correct selection
Facial features
Head and face shapes
Hairstyle
Hair density
Hair growth patterns and skin elasticity

Create a range of facial hair shapes

Introduction
Preparing the client's facial hair before cutting
Methods of cutting beards/moustaches
Removing unwanted hair from the outside of the perimeter line
Five in a row
Facial cutting techniques
Scissor over comb

Clipper over comb
Freehand cutting
Moustache and beard shapes
Full beard and moustache trim 1
Full beard and moustache trim 2
Cutting partial beard and moustache effect
Cutting a moustache look
Client care

Provide aftercare advice

Introduction

Products
Worksheet – Provide aftercare advice
Online multiple choice quiz

12.1 Working safely

As with other services, health and safety requirements must always be followed when cutting facial hair. Much of the content in this section you may have studied during your Level 2 training but we recommend that you take another look to refresh your knowledge.

Preparing the client for facial cutting

It is important to gown the client effectively prior to cutting facial hair. This is to protect the client's clothes and to ensure that the client is comfortable. Hair cuttings are extremely prickly when they go down the back of the neck and can penetrate the skin causing an infection. Cuttings are also very difficult to remove from clothes.

Protective equipment varies from salon to salon but your salon may use the following:

- gown covering all clothing ensuring there are no gaps
- towel fastened at the back of the client
- cotton wool strip or neck wool placed around client's neck.

After the client has been gowned, their eyes should be covered with dampened eye pads to ensure that no clippings enter the eyes. Do not have too much bulk from clothes and towels around the neck; this restricts the accuracy when cutting and in some cases the mobility of the client's neck.

Safety first

Chapter 2 covers health and safety working methods in more detail. Refer to this unit if necessary.

Safety first

Hair cuttings are extremely prickly when they go down the back of the neck, and can penetrate the skin causing an infection.

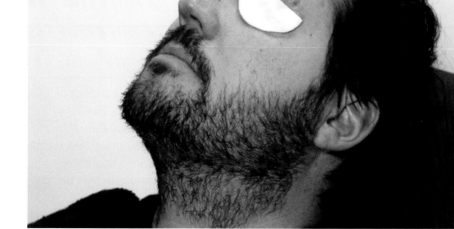

Figure 12.1 The client should be protected from hair clippings

Comfort during cutting facial hair

When cutting men's facial hair, the client must have their head tilted back in order for you to work safely and accurately. The barbering chair has a reclining facility and headrest allowing the client to be comfortable in this position. The client should have both feet squarely on the footrest which will help both the client to be comfortable and you to work safely. Your own comfort during cutting should be considered as well. Check that your posture is correct, ensuring that your client's seat is at the correct height for you to work.

Figure 12.2 The headrest allows the client to tilt their head back comfortably

Keep work area tidy

Ensure that your work area is tidy and free from clutter.

After cutting always remember to sweep the hair cuttings off the floor and dispose of them in the appropriate place.

Tools and equipment

Scissors

These come in a variety of materials such as stainless steel, with metal or plastic handles. They also come in a variety of designs and prices. Picking scissors up and holding them is the best way to see if they are suitable. It is important that they feel comfortable. Scissors should always be clean and sharp. Before sterilising remember to remove all loose hairs. The blades should be sprayed with sterilising spray or wiped carefully with sterile wipes before being placed in the ultraviolet cabinet for the correct length of time according to the manufacturer's instructions.

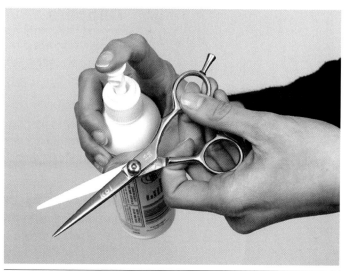

Figure 12.3 Different types of scissors

Figure 12.4 Sterilising scissors

Online activity 12.1 **www**

Round the board

Combs

Combs used for barbering are different to those used in hairdressing. The barbering comb has a tapered edge and is more flexible than the hairdressing comb. The length of the comb should be based around how comfortable it is for you to hold and work with. To clean, combs should be washed in water with detergent and then placed in sterilising solution for the correct length of time according to the manufacturer's instructions.

Key information

The barbering comb has a tapered edge and is more flexible than the hairdressing comb.

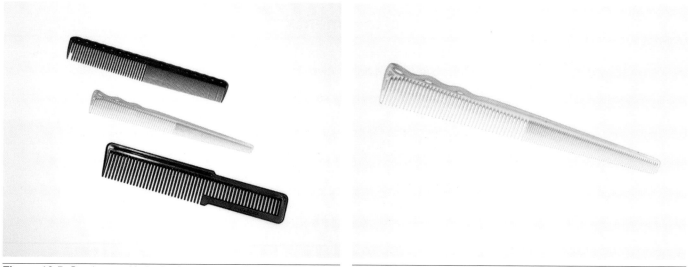

Figure 12.5 Combs used in barbering

Figure 12.6 Barbering comb

Clippers

Always follow the manufacturer's instructions when using clippers so that you use them safely. When in use the bottom blade remains still whilst the top blade moves across it very quickly to cut the hair.

Ensure that you check the alignment of the clipper blades before use. Small adjustments can be made by loosening the small screws that are positioned underneath. Remember to oil clippers using clipper oil after every use to keep them lubricated and clean. This also prolongs the life of the blades.

After use, clean away hairs from the clippers. Sometimes the blades must be removed to clean away hair. If this is not done, the clippers may not work properly, causing discomfort to the client. All repairs to electric clippers should be carried out by a qualified electrician.

Safety first ⚠️

All repairs to electric clippers should be carried out by a qualified electrician.

Figure 12.7 Clippers and attachments

Clipper attachments

Clipper attachment sizes start at grade 1 and go up to grade 8 for cutting hair. This table shows the amount of hair that is left for each clipper grade.

Table 12.1 Grades of clipper attachment

Clipper grade	Length of hair left
1	3 mm / $\frac{1}{8}$ inch
2	6 mm / $\frac{1}{4}$ inch
3	10 mm / $\frac{3}{8}$ inch
4	13 mm / $\frac{1}{2}$ inch
5	16 mm / $\frac{5}{8}$ inch
6	19 mm / $\frac{3}{4}$ inch
7	22 mm / $\frac{7}{8}$ inch
8	25 mm / 1 inch

Towels and gowns

All towels and gowns should be clean and sterile for each client to prevent cross-infection of parasitic, viral, fungal and bacterial diseases. These include:

- pediculosis capitis
- herpes simplex
- tinea capitis
- impetigo.

Online activity 12.2

Correct selection

Figure 12.8 Towels and gowns should be clean and sterile

Consultation

Before any service begins the barber must find out what the client wants or needs. The consultation is used to ensure the client's wishes are interpreted accurately and the desired look achieved. It is essential to be factual, honest, tactful, sincere, direct and clear. Visual aids will help the client to show you the effect that he would like to have, for example men's style magazines or pictures from the Internet. This is especially helpful if the client wants a look that is avant-garde. Keeping up to date with the trends in facial hair styles will help to recommend a particular look for the client.

> **Definitions**
>
> **Pediculosis capitis:** Also known as head lice. Tiny insects that are spread by head-to-head contact.
>
> **Herpes simplex:** A viral infection affecting the skin and nervous system.
>
> **Tinea capitis:** Fungal infection that is contagious.
>
> **Impetigo:** Contagious bacterial skin disease.

Figure 12.9 Find out what the client needs

> **Definition**
>
> **Avant-garde:** A term used to describe artwork that breaks away from tradition.

Factors influencing the service

You should identify any factors that may influence the client's choice of facial style.

These include:

- facial features
- head and face shapes
- hairstyle
- hair density
- hair growth patterns
- skin elasticity.

See Chapter 3 for information on adverse skin conditions including infections or infestations that may prevent you from performing this service.

www Online activity 12.3

Correct selection

Facial features

Generally the larger the client's facial features, the thicker the beard or moustache can be. If the client has finer features then they should have a smaller design. This is shown here, with the client having a small mouth and so a moustache that is short and narrow would best suit him.

If the client has a large prominent nose, a thicker moustache would suit him.

Any facial scarring can be hidden with beards or moustaches.

If the client has any facial piercings, then either ask the client to remove them or take extra care when combing and cutting around these areas.

Figure 12.10 A thick beard will suit a client with large facial features

Figure 12.11 A thin moustache suits a client with small features

Figure 12.12 A thick moustache suits a client with a prominent nose

Head and face shapes

Men with square faces can soften their look by having beards or moustaches that are rounded.

Figure 12.13 Rounded beards tend to suit square faces

Round faces can be lengthened by choosing beard designs that have angles and lines instead of curves.

Figure 12.14 Square beards tend to suit round faces

Oval shaped faces tend to suit any facial style. A beard or moustache should be chosen that enhances the client's features.

Figure 12.15 Oval faces tend to look good with any style

Small faces should keep small facial hair designs that are cut close and are the same in length.

Figure 12.16 Small hair designs suit small faces

If the client has a wide head, a beard that is full and long will flatter him. It should be cut close at the side and longer at the chin.

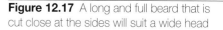

Figure 12.17 A long and full beard that is cut close at the sides will suit a wide head

Hairstyle

The beard or moustache the client wishes to have should complement his hairstyle. A client with little or no hair will look good with a beard or moustache that is small and close cut, whereas a client with thick long hair should wear a larger beard. Work together with the client to find a style that suits him and he is happy with.

Figure 12.18 A beard or moustache that is small and close cut will suit a client who has no hair

Figure 12.19 A large beard is suitable for a client with long, thick hair

Hair density

The client's choice of style will be influenced by the density of facial hair. If a client has thick facial hair, they may not be able to have a narrow, fine moustache. The density will also affect the tools and techniques that are used, e.g. clippers may need to be used instead of scissors for a thick beard.

Figure 12.20 The density of the client's facial hair will affect his style

Hair growth patterns and skin elasticity

Check to see if there are any hair growth patterns in the client's facial hair. This might affect the way it is cut. For example, if the client has any whorls, the hair may need to be cut close to the skin or left at a longer length so that they are unnoticed. This is also the case if there are any thinning or missing areas. As the skin ages, it will lose its elasticity; therefore it will be less taut. To avoid cutting the skin, it must be pulled slightly to create tension.

Activity to complete WWW

Find out your expected service times for cutting beards and moustaches and make a note here:

12.2 Create a range of facial hair shapes

This section covers the skills needed to cut facial hair to create the desired look. Your consultation will have established the service that you will be providing, but ensure that throughout the cutting process your client is happy with what you are doing. This may mean uncovering their eyes to check they are happy with the design you are creating.

Preparing the client's facial hair before cutting

You should untangle the facial hair before cutting. Then the hair should be cleansed as this will make the cut easier. If the client is having another service which involves shampooing, this can be done at the same time. If there is no other service, the client can wash his face and beard at the front wash basin. Alternatively cleansers or cleansing wipes can be used.

Figure 12.21 Cleansing the client's beard

Methods of cutting beards/moustaches

Definition

Systematic: To complete in a set order/follow a set system.

When cutting beards and moustaches, it will be easier if you work in a systematic manner. That way the pattern you are following will be clear. Working from either side or the middle, it is helpful to cut channels of hair which follow the guidelines you are creating. Remember to try to follow the client's natural hairline on the face. If you don't do this the style will look out of balance and uneven. It will also be difficult for the client to maintain.

It is important to check the balance of the shaping throughout to ensure that you are creating an even finish. Moustaches are usually trimmed with the scissors for better control and to stop the clippers vibrating and tickling the client. This may make them pull away.

Key information

It is important to check the balance of the shaping throughout to ensure that you are creating an even finish.

Removing unwanted hair from the outside of the perimeter line

To finish the look, make sure that any hair that is not wanted on the outside of the perimeter line is removed. This is done once the client is happy with the shape you have created. The clippers are inverted and the edge used to mark a clear line. Once this is done they are turned back around and the unwanted hair is removed. If necessary, gently pull the skin so that it is taut to get a closer cut.

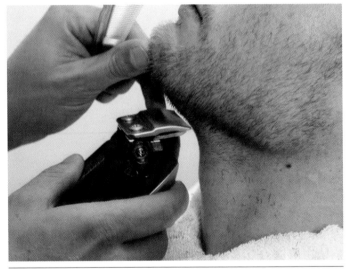

Figure 12.22 Marking out an edge of the perimeter line

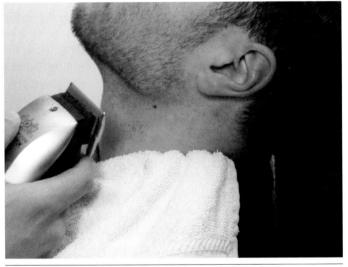

Figure 12.23 Remove unwanted hair outside the edge

Definition

Inverted: Turned upside down or in the opposite direction.

WWW **Online activity 12.4**

Five in a row

Facial cutting techniques

These include:

- scissor over comb
- clipper over comb
- freehand.

Scissor over comb

Used when the hair is required to be very short and finely graduated. When using this cutting method a smooth flowing movement is required to avoid 'steps' in the hair. The comb is placed against the skin and the hair cut as the comb is moved away from the face.

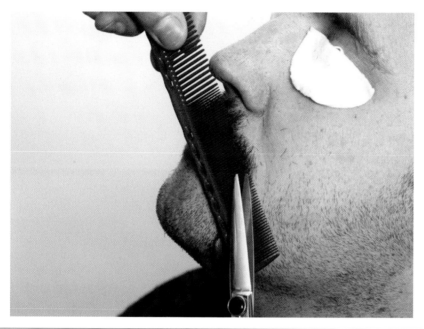

Figure 12.24 Scissor over comb technique

Clipper over comb

This eliminates the hard work from the scissor over comb technique. Clipper over comb is used for removing bulk and shaping beards and moustaches. Place the comb and hold at the appropriate angle under a section of hair. Glide the clippers across the comb. Repeat this until the required length is achieved.

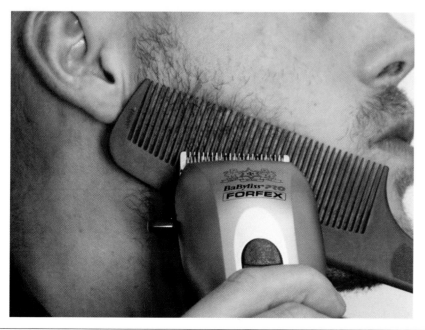

Figure 12.25 Clipper over comb technique

Freehand cutting

When you cut the beard or moustache without holding it with the fingers, this is known as freehand cutting. It is usually carried out to tidy the beard or moustache once the main bulk has been removed.

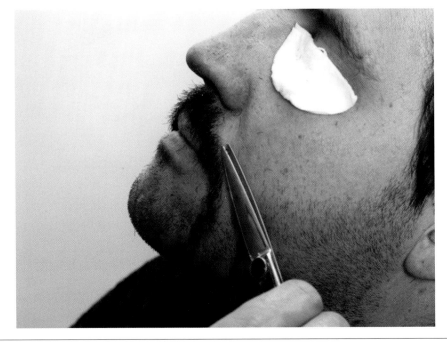

Figure 12.26 Freehand cutting technique

Moustache and beard shapes

Here are some examples of beard and moustache shapes that the client may wish you to cut and shape:

Figure 12.27 Beard and moustache shapes

Full beard and moustache trim

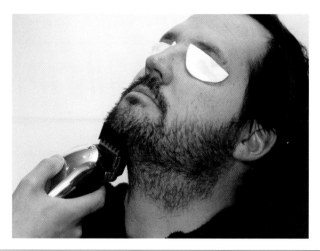

Figure 12.28 After the client is protected and seated correctly in a comfortable position, the beard is combed through to untangle. Using the clippers with attachment, shorten the beard according to the client's wishes

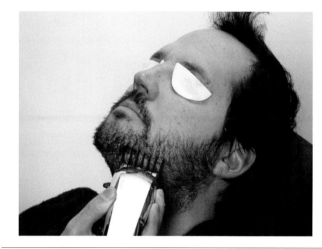

Figure 12.29 Move around the face in a methodical manner

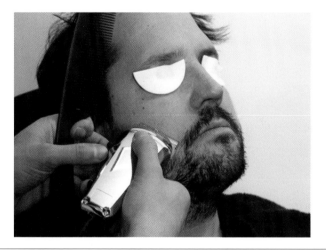

Figure 12.30 Once the beard has been shortened, remove unwanted hair around the edge

Figure 12.31 Invert the clippers and use the edge to mark a clear line before removing the unwanted hair below the line, holding the skin with the required tension

Figure 12.32 The finished look

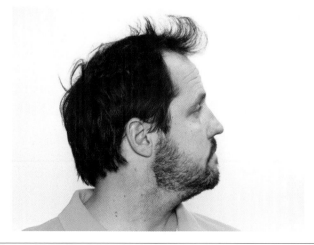

Figure 12.33 The finished look

Cutting partial beard and moustache effect

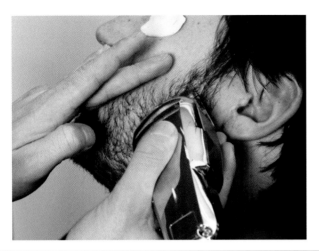

Figure 12.34 Once the beard has been shortened to the client's desired length the hair outside the beard area is removed. The skin is held taut in required areas

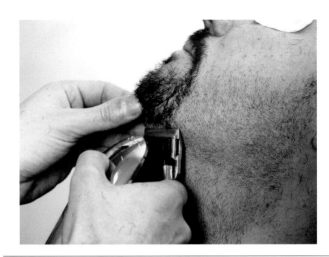

Figure 12.35 Use the clippers to shape the beard

Figure 12.36 Finished look

Cutting a moustache look

Figure 12.37 Remove the unwanted hair outside the moustache area. Ask the client to purse his lips to create tension when needed

Figure 12.38 Use the scissor over comb technique to cut close to the skin

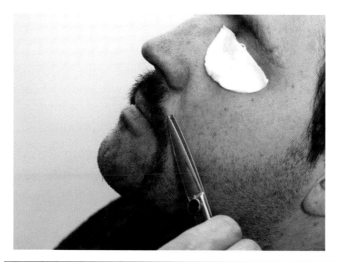

Figure 12.39 Use the freehand technique to tidy up the edge around the moustache

Figure 12.40 The finished look

Client care

After cutting, remove any loose clippings of hair from the face and neck. Check with the client that he is happy with the finished look.

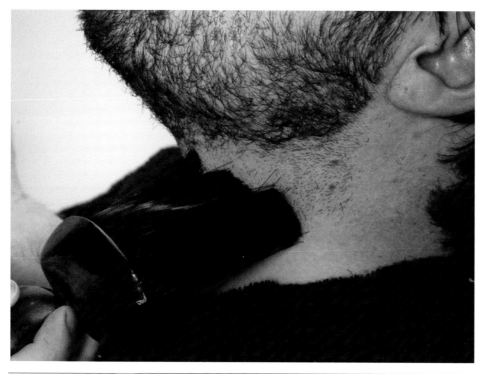

Figure 12.41 Remove loose hair clippings

12.3 Provide aftercare advice

An important part of this service is to give the client aftercare advice.

You should explain to the client how often he should return to the salon to maintain his beard and/or moustache. This will depend on the length; the average rate of growth of hair is 1.25 cm per month, so it is likely between 3

and 5 weeks. Clients with shorter styles will need to return to the salon more often than those with longer styles. This is particularly relevant for clients with moustaches as they will grow over the upper lip quickly.

The client should be given advice on tidying up the perimeter of his beard or moustache as it is likely he will wish to do this himself. This will usually be carried out using nail scissors or electric razors. The client's lifestyle must be taken into consideration when creating a style that he can maintain.

Figure 12.42 Advise the client which products can be used

Products

Advise the client which products can be used at home. This should be based on the factors that influence the service. Explain to the client the benefits of exfoliating the skin. This will remove dead skin cells from the surface layer of the epidermis and so stimulate blood circulation, improving the condition of the skin (elasticity). If this is carried out regularly the client is less likely to suffer from skin infections, e.g. ingrowing hairs.

Definition

Ingrowing hair: This condition occurs when a hair curls around and grows back into itself or the skin.

12.4 Worksheets

You can carry out the worksheets during your study of a chapter or unit, or at the end. An example is presented here and there are more online. If your college or company is registered with ATT Training, lots more are available. Write your answers directly in the book, but only if you own it of course – if it is a library or college book, use a separate piece of paper!

12.4.1 Provide aftercare advice

There are some keys points to be considered when giving your clients aftercare advice.

Answer these questions:

1. What is the average rate of facial hair growth per month?

2. When should you suggest that your client return to the salon?

3. What factors will have an impact on when the client should return to the salon?

4. What types of styles would require the client to return to the salon sooner?

5. Should you give your client advice on how to tidy up his beard or moustache at home? If not, why not?

6. The client's lifestyle should be taken into consideration when creating a style. What factors may influence this decision?

12.5 Assessment

Well done! If you have studied all the content of this unit you may be ready to test your knowledge.

Check out the 'Preparing for assessments' section in Chapter 1 if you have not already done so, and always remember:

- You can only do your best if you have. . .
  - studied hard
  - completed the activities
  - completed the worksheets
  - practised, practised, practised
  - and then revised!

 **Now carry out the online multiple-choice quiz**

. . . and good luck in the final exam, which will be arranged by your tutor/assessor.

Creatively cut hair using a combination of barbering techniques

This chapter covers the NVQ/SVQ unit GB8, Creatively cut hair using a combination of barbering techniques.

This unit teaches you how to restyle men's hair using a wide range of cutting techniques that you have learnt previously. Men have become more interested in styles that are creative so it is particularly relevant for you to improve your skills in this area in order to meet clients' requirements.

In this chapter you will learn about:

- maintaining effective and safe methods of working when cutting hair
- creatively restyle men's hair
- providing aftercare advice.

CHAPTER 13 CREATIVELY CUT HAIR USING A COMBINATION OF BARBERING TECHNIQUES: CONTENTS, SCREENS AND ACTIVITIES

Key:
Sections from the book are set in this colour
Screens available online are set in this colour
Online activity screens are set in this colour

Working safely

Creatively restyling men's hair

Provide aftercare advice

13.1 Working safely

Much of the health and safety information related to cutting men's hair has been covered during your Level 2 training but we recommend you take another look to refresh your knowledge. Chapter 2 covers health and safety working methods in more detail. Refer to this unit if necessary.

Preparing a client for a haircut

It is important to gown the client effectively prior to cutting the hair. This is to protect the client's clothes and to ensure that the client is comfortable. Hair cuttings are extremely prickly when they go down the back of the neck and can penetrate the skin causing an infection. Cuttings are also very difficult to remove from clothes.

Figure 13.1 Gown the client

Key information

Do not have too much bulk from clothes and towels around the neck; this restricts the accuracy when cutting and in some cases the mobility of the client's neck.

Comfort during cutting

Whilst cutting the client's hair, it is important for you to move around the client's head. However, the client's comfort should be considered at all times. Their back should be positioned right to the back of the chair and as flat as possible. They should have both feet on the footrest or the floor. Not only will this be a more comfortable position for the client but it also enables you to create a balanced hairstyle. Your own comfort during cutting should be considered as well. Check that your posture is correct, ensuring that your client's seat is at the correct height for you to work. Ensure that your work area is tidy and free from clutter and that your equipment is pre-selected and ready to use.

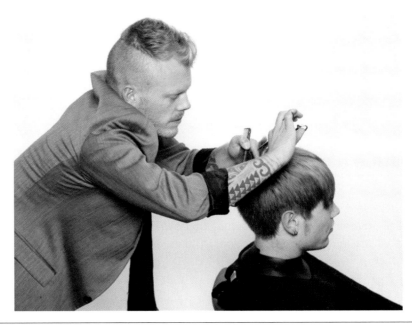

Figure 13.2 Incorrect posture

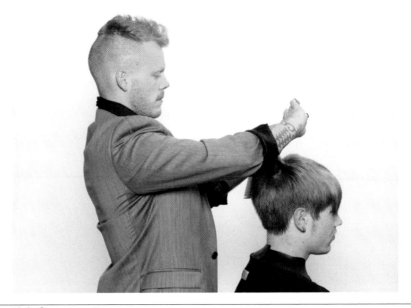

Figure 13.3 Correct posture

Dispose of waste immediately

After cutting always remember to sweep the hair cuttings off the floor and dispose of them in the appropriate place.

Tools and Equipment

Scissors

These come in a variety of materials such as stainless steel, with metal or plastic handles. They also come in a variety of designs and price. Picking scissors up and holding them is the best way to see if they are suitable. It is important that they feel comfortable. Scissors should always be clean and sharp. Before sterilising remember to remove all loose hairs.

Figure 13.4 Different types of scissors

Figure 13.5 Pick scissors up to see if they are comfortable to hold

Figure 13.6 Remove any loose hairs

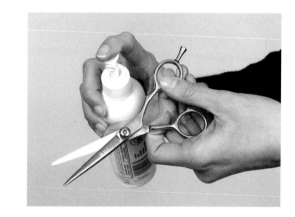

Figure 13.7 Sterilising scissors

Thinning scissors

There are scissors specifically designed for thinning the hair. They have one or possibly two blades that look like the teeth on a comb. The teeth of the blades are sharp and cut the hair. The gaps between the teeth just allow the hair to pass through without removing any hair at all. The size of the gap determines how much hair is removed.

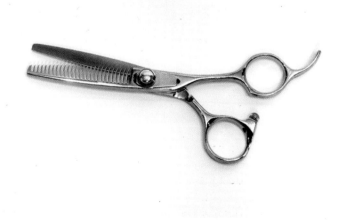

Figure 13.8 Thinning scissors with one blade serrated

Figure 13.9 And with two blades serrated

Razors

The main types of razors used are cut-throat razors, safety razors and shapers. Cut-throat or open razors have a blade that folds into the handle. Safety razors have a disposable blade and so these can be changed between clients. This makes the service more hygienic. Shapers also have disposable blades and are used for cutting hair. They are not used for shaving.

Figure 13.10 Cut-throat razor

Figure 13.11 Safety razor

Definition

Disposable: Intended for use once and then thrown away.

Razors can only be used on wet hair. When used on dry hair they tear and shred the cuticle leaving the cortex frayed and exposed. It is also uncomfortable for the client. Salons using razor blades must dispose of them in a container such as a sharps box.

Figure 13.12 Dispose of razors in a box like this

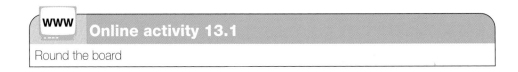

WWW Online activity 13.1

Round the board

Clippers

Always follow the manufacturer's instructions when using clippers so that you use them safely. When in use the bottom blade remains still whilst the top blade moves across it very quickly to cut the hair. Ensure that you check the alignment of the clipper blades before use. Small adjustments can be made by loosening the small screws that are positioned underneath. Remember to oil clippers using clipper oil after every use to keep them lubricated and clean. This also prolongs the life of the blades. After use, clean away hairs from the clippers. The blades must sometimes be removed to clean away hair. If this is not done, the clippers may not work properly, causing discomfort to the client. All repairs to electric clippers should be carried out by a qualified electrician.

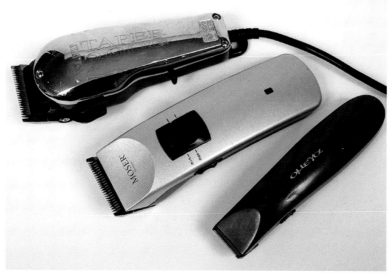

 **Safety first**

Always follow the manufacturer's instructions when using clippers so that you use them safely.

Figure 13.13 Electric clippers

Clipper attachments

Figure 13.14 Clippers with attachments

Clipper attachment sizes start at grade 1 and go up to grade 8 for cutting hair. This table shows the amount of hair that is left for each clipper grade.

Table 13.1 Grades of clipper attachment

Clipper grade	Length of hair left
1	3 mm / $\frac{1}{8}$ inch
2	6 mm / $\frac{1}{4}$ inch
3	10 mm / $\frac{3}{8}$ inch
4	13 mm / $\frac{1}{2}$ inch
5	16 mm / $\frac{5}{8}$ inch
6	19 mm / $\frac{3}{4}$ inch
7	22 mm / $\frac{7}{8}$ inch
8	25 mm / 1 inch

Finishing products

The following finishing products are used for men's styling:

- gels
- sprays
- waxes
- creams.

Refer to Chapter 9 for more information on the effects they achieve.

Consultation

Before any service begins the hairdresser must find out what the client wants or needs. The consultation is used to ensure the client's wishes are interpreted accurately and the desired look achieved. It is essential to be factual, honest, tactful, sincere, direct and clear.

> **Key information**
>
> To prevent wastage of products, only use the amount needed according to the manufacturer's instructions.

Figure 13.15 Ask the client what he would like

Analyse the hair and scalp

Prior to all barbering tasks it is necessary to analyse the hair and scalp. This includes a visual and physical examination. The hair should be combed through to check for factors that will influence the client's choice of style.

There are factors that will influence the client's choice of style. The following have been covered in Chapter 3 (refer to this if necessary). They are:

- hair growth patterns
- hair density and texture
- hair elasticity.

The following factors are specific to men's styling:

- male pattern baldness
- added hair
- head and face shapes.

> **Key information**
>
> See Chapter 3 for for information on hair and scalp disorders or contraindications to the hairdressing service (including infections and infestations).

Figure 13.16 Always check the client's hair and scalp

Online activity 13.2 **WWW**

correct
you
the
this
statements
choose
from
Can
?
list

Well Done!

Figure 13.17 Online activity screen

Correct selection

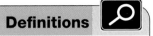

Male pattern baldness

Before cutting men's hair, it is essential to look for any signs of male pattern balding (MPB). The cause of this condition is believed to be hereditary and due to an excess level of the hormone testosterone.

Alopecia totalis is a total baldness of the head. When the baldness starts as a small round patch that spreads outwards, this is known as alopecia areata. The hair grows back from the middle of the balding patch and there may be more than one patch at any time.

Your advice will depend on the stage of baldness. If there is a slow loss of hair, reassurance should be given and the different styling options explained. If there is a great deal of hair loss, there will be a limited number of styles that you can create.

Figure 13.18 Patterns in male baldness

Added hair

If your client has a toupee, the hairstyle you create must allow for this. It must be a balanced style, blending the client's real hair into the added hair. If your client has a full hairpiece it is likely he will wish to have his hair short underneath.

Head and face shapes

The client may have the following head or face shape:

- oval
- square
- oblong
- round.

The oval shaped face is considered to be the perfect shape that suits any style. However, many people have differing features and it is important to choose the hairstyle to suit each client's face shape and features.

Men with a square facial shape tend to appear masculine looking, with a strong angular jawline and square hairline. This type of face shape enables a hairstyle that gives a classic traditional look for short hair.

Figure 13.19 Square faces appear masculine looking

Most hairstyles work well with an oblong face as it is similar to an oval shape.

Figure 13.20 Oblong faces appear to suit most styles

Figure 13.21 Long hair or volume on top of the head suits round faces

If your client has a round face, a hairstyle that is flat at the sides with volume on top will flatter him. Long hair will also give the illusion of length.

Large ears that protrude need to be covered for a flattering effect.

If the client has a big nose or broken nose a centre parting will exaggerate this. Choose an asymmetric style. This will be more flattering.

A fringe will achieve the best effect for a client with a high forehead or receding hairline.

A short stocky neck requires a softer hairstyle which is more flattering to the client.

Activity to complete www

Find out your expected service times for restyling men's hair and make a note here:

13.2 Creatively restyling men's hair

In this section you will learn how to perform haircuts that include different techniques of cutting. You will be creating many different looks.

Establishing the client's choice of cut

Before cutting hair, a great way of establishing the client's choice of cut is to look through magazines or style books during the consultation. Look at what the client is wearing before he has his gown put on to establish the desired style. Ask questions related to their lifestyle. All information gathered at this stage will help you to establish a choice of cut.

Using your communication skills, recommend a style based on their preference and the relevant factors, e.g. face shape, growth patterns, current style, hair condition and type. Establish with the client the amount of hair to be cut. Always make sure that you repeat to the client what you understand to be his wishes. Confirm this once more before commencing the cut.

Key information

Look at what the client is wearing before he has his gown put on to establish the desired style.

Figure 13.22 Ask the client how much hair he would like cut off

Wet and dry cutting

The benefits of cutting hair when it is dry include:

- any growth patterns and movement to the hair can be seen clearly
- a quicker haircut can be carried out
- the client's desired length is easily achieved.

Figure 13.23 Cutting dry hair

The benefits of cutting hair when it is wet include:

- combing and managing the hair will be easier
- sections will be clearer
- more accurate and controlled cut will be possible
- any curl to the hair will be visible.

Wet hair will have more elasticity so needs to be held with less tension or you may cut the hair too short. It is important to ensure the hair stays damp when wet cutting, especially when using a razor.

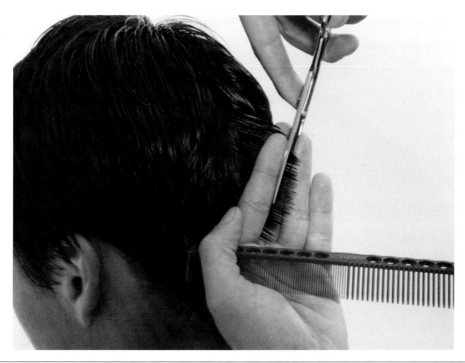

 **Key information**

It is important to ensure the hair stays damp when wet cutting, especially when using a razor.

Figure 13.24 Cutting wet hair

WWW **Online activity 13.3**

Correct selection

Cutting techniques and effects

These include:

- club cutting
- scissor and clipper over comb
- freehand
- thinning, tapering and texturising
- fading
- razor cutting
- graduating, layering and disconnecting.

Club cutting

Each section of hair is cut straight across bluntly, usually with scissors, but this can also be achieved with clippers. The hair mesh is cut straight across to produce level ends.

Figure 13.25 Club cutting technique

Scissor and clipper over comb

Used when the hair is required to be very short and finely graduated. When using this cutting method a smooth flowing movement is required to avoid 'steps' in the hair. Keep the head up in a sitting position. Use the points of the scissors to lift a section of hair. Place a comb under the section of hair. Glide the comb in an upward direction. Follow the comb with the scissors and carefully cut the hair to the required length. Open and close the scissors rapidly clipping away at the length.

The clipper over comb technique eliminates the hard work from the scissor over comb technique. Place the comb and hold at the appropriate angle under a section of hair. Glide the clippers across the comb. Repeat this until the required length is achieved.

Figure 13.26 Scissor over comb technique

Figure 13.27 Clipper over comb technique

Freehand cutting

This is the way of cutting the hair without holding it with the fingers. It is mainly used when cutting fringes, around the perimeter edges near the ears and for trimming hair around growth patterns. Comb the hair into place and then cut freehand without using tension on the hair. By not using tension on the hair when it is dry, it gives a better indication of where the hair will sit.

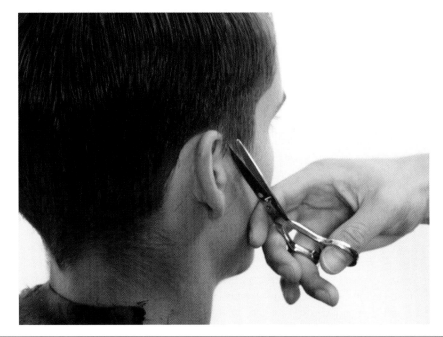

Figure 13.28 Freehand cutting

Thinning, tapering and texturising

Thinning removes bulk from the hair. Many cutting techniques can be used to do this, not only the use of thinning scissors. It can be carried out on wet or dry hair.

Figure 13.29 Thinning the hair using thinning scissors

Another method to remove bulk and volume is tapering. It can also be known as feathering. The hair is cut to produce a tapered point.

Figure 13.30 Tapering using a razor

Texturising involves using the points of the scissors to break up the points of the hair. This will create texture in hair that has been club cut. Another technique for texturing is called brick cutting.

Figure 13.31 Texturising

Fading

This technique is carried out using clippers. Very short hair at the bottom is blended into longer hair at the top of the head. This produces a haircut where the length of the hair increases or decreases gradually without any lines.

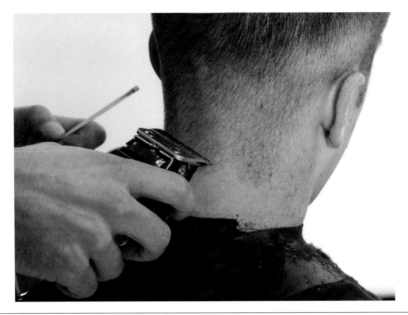

Figure 13.32 Fading the hair

WWW **Online activity 13.4**

Five in a row

Razor cutting

This effect is similar to tapering. The razor is sliced down the hair to remove bulk and volume. The amount of force with which the razor cutting is carried out will determine how much hair is removed.

Figure 13.33 Razor cutting

Graduating, layering and disconnecting

Most men's haircuts will be graduated, with the hair being cut to different lengths throughout. The angle that is produced between the long and short ends of the hair is often referred to as the 'graduation'.

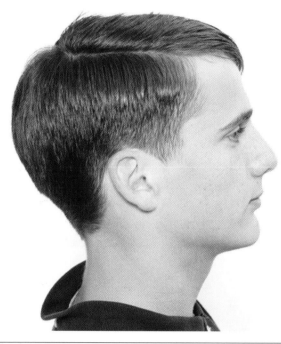

Figure 13.34 Graduated hair

Again, most men's haircuts will be layered. The uniform layer cut is a common technique, where the hair is elevated at 90 degrees to the scalp.

Figure 13.35 Uniform layer haircut being carried out

Disconnecting the hair means that the hair is cut to leave long and short sections. It gives a dramatic look.

Figure 13.36 Disconnected hair

Outline and neckline shapes

When creating a haircut, you should try to use the natural hairline as the perimeter. Doing this will enable the style to look balanced. If the perimeter is above the natural hairline, then once the hair grows back, it will look untidy. If this is not possible, e.g. if the client has a very short style with an even growth around the hairline, it should be defined. The look will be less harsh if the nape line looks natural.

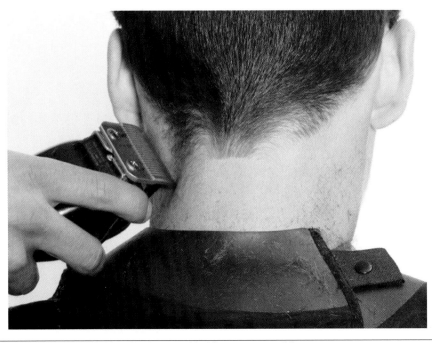

Figure 13.37 Work with the client's natural hairline to ensure tidiness

The neckline could be shaped in the following ways:

- rounded
- squared
- tapered.

A rounded neckline takes the square corners off and it has the benefit of adding balance to a wide neck.

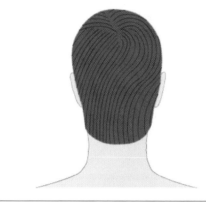

Figure 13.38 A rounded neckline

A square neckline has the appearance of a hard line against the neck. It should be shaved to follow the natural hairline as closely as possible. This kind of neckline will add width to a slim neck. The disadvantage is that when the hair grows back it can appear untidy.

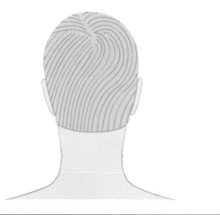

Figure 13.39 A square neckline

A tapered hairline follows the natural hairline. A wide neck will appear slim with this neckline and as the hair grows back it will not look untidy.

Figure 13.40 A tapered neckline

Cutting angles and guidelines

You should be aware of the cutting angles you are using throughout the haircut. The holding and cutting angle will affect the balance and amount of graduation it has. A guideline is the first section of hair that is cut and to which the next section/s are subsequently cut. The number of guidelines will depend on how simple or complex the haircut is.

Figure 13.41 The angle to which the hair is held will affect the amount of graduation

Natural fall

As mentioned previously, when preparing the client's hair, it is important to look for the hair's natural fall. This also applies during the haircut, as you must always work with the client's natural fall, e.g. partings, nape whorls, etc. This will make the style easier to manage for the client.

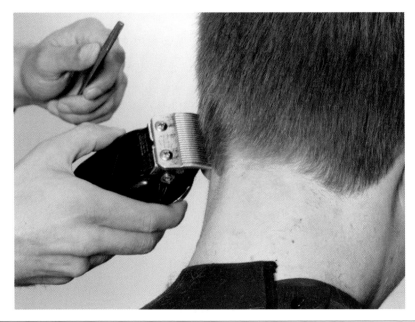

Figure 13.42 Work with the client's natural fall

Cross-checking

At the end of a haircut and possibly during the process, it is important to check the cut you have created. You do this by holding sections of hair out at right angles to the original sections. This enables you to see how accurate the cut is. If you find any areas that are not even, you can cut the hair accordingly.

Dealing with problems during cutting

If a thorough and accurate consultation is carried out, you shouldn't really make any cutting mistakes, but if you do you should know how to deal with them. An example of this is if you are cutting the hair and you find that there is a growth pattern that stops the hair from lying correctly. This should have been picked up from the consultation during analysis but to overcome the problem you should change the style to suit the hair growth. Another common problem that occurs is that you may feel that you have cut one side of a symmetrical haircut too short. You should stop and check with your fingers, looking in the mirror at the same time. Only if the cut still seems unbalanced, you should make adjustments as necessary.

Key information

If a thorough and accurate consultation is carried out, you shouldn't really make any cutting mistakes, but if you do you should know how to deal with them.

Figure 13.43 Carrying out an accurate consultation should stop problems occurring during cutting

Online activity 13.5 **www**

Round the board

Preparing the client's hair before cutting

If the client has products on his hair, e.g. styling gel, the hair must be washed to remove it. If not the hair will be sticky and it will be hard to cut accurately. It is always best to wash the hair, even if carrying out a dry cut, for this reason.

It will also help you to see the natural fall of the hair. Before any haircut, the hair must be combed through to untangle. This is very important as you need to be able to see any growth patterns and natural partings.

Figure 13.44 Washing the client's hair

Figure 13.45 Comb the hair through before a cut

Creating a combination of looks

You should be able to create a variety of looks using a combination of techniques. A traditional look is a look that has been popular for many years, for example short back and sides. A current look is a look that is fashionable at the time. It is popular with people who change their hairstyle often. The consultation that you have carried out with your client will establish which type of look your client wishes to have.

Figure 13.46 Traditional look

Creating a fade haircut with a flat top

Figure 13.47 After gowning in the appropriate manner and combing the hair through, section both sides of the hair from temple to crown

Figure 13.48 Using clippers with the highest grade attachment, move in an upwards direction at the sides. Don't forget to hold the client's ears back if necessary

Figure 13.49 Move in sections to the back of the head

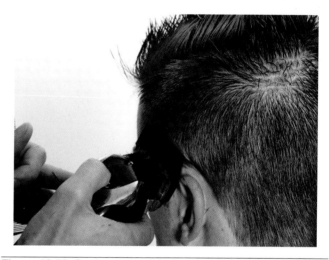

Figure 13.50 Continue around the head to the other side

Figure 13.51 Change the clippers to a shorter grade and clip the bottom half of the head. This will create a line which will be blended in later

Figure 13.52 Join the back into the sides of the haircut by cutting the hair at a 45 degree angle using the scissors

Figure 13.53 Follow the guideline over the top of the head, through the central profile parting to the front of the head

Figure 13.54 Move to the back of the head and take sections across the central profile parting. Club cut the hair to the guideline in the middle. Move towards the front of the head, taking sections of the parting

Figure 13.55 To create a square look for the haircut, the hair between short and long at the sides is held at 90 degrees with the scissors and cut straight down

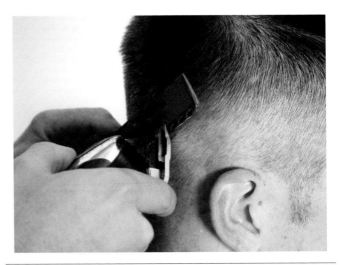

Figure 13.56 Use a clipper over comb technique to blend the area between the different clipper lengths

Figure 13.57 Holding a large comb flat to the head, blend the short hair into the long hair. Cross-check the haircut

Figure 13.58 Use the point cutting technique to texturise the hair on the top of the head

Figure 13.59 The faded haircut is then finished off using clippers first of all in an upturned position, taking minimal amounts of hair off. Then the blades are put in the original position and the hairline is faded out

Figure 13.60 The hair is washed to remove all the short clippings and then dried. Products are applied to finish the look

The finished style incorporated the following techniques and effects:

* club cutting
* clippers with attachments
* clipper over comb
* fading
* texturising
* graduating.

Creating a disconnected haircut

Figure 13.61 After gowning in the appropriate manner and combing the hair through, section both sides of the hair from temple to crown. Section the front inch of the hair forwards

Figure 13.62 Using clippers with the highest grade attachment, move straight up the occipital bone but stop before reaching the crown. This creates the disconnection

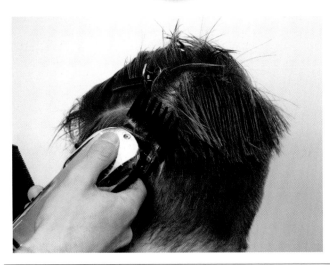

Figure 13.63 Move in sections around to the other side of the head

Figure 13.64 Using the clippers with a lower grade attachment, blend in the graduated hair below the longer disconnected hair

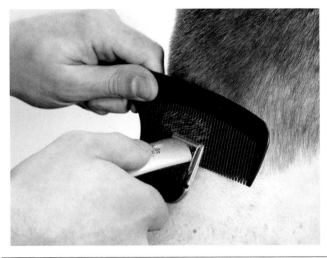

Figure 13.65 Using trimmers, carry out the clipper over comb technique to tidy up the hairline

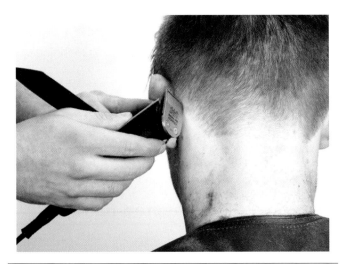

Figure 13.66 Invert the trimmers to mark out the neckline

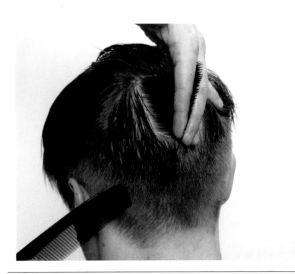

Figure 13.67 To maintain the length at the top of the head, uniform layers are created. The hair is elevated at 45 degrees to create the guideline

Figure 13.68 This guideline is followed through the middle of the central profile parting

Figure 13.69 Taking sections across the central profile parting, club cut to the guideline which can be seen in the middle

Figure 13.70 When the hair in the fringe area is reached, elevate back so that length is maintained

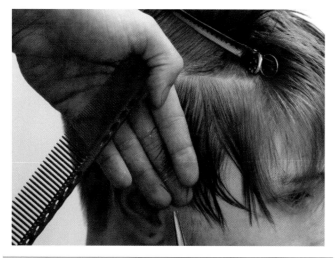

Figure 13.71 At the sides of the head, the hair in front of the ears is combed forwards at a 45 degree angle away from the head. To blend the long hair at the sides into the short hair to create a graduation, the hair is combed back on itself in sections, and cut moving from the bottom of the head to the top

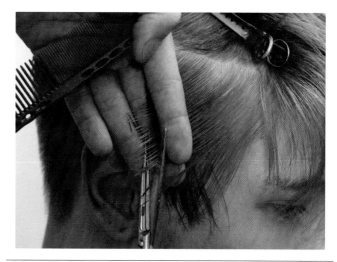

Figure 13.72 Follow the guideline to the front of the head

Figure 13.73 Graduation effect created at the sides

Figure 13.74 Dry the hair and texturise by point cutting

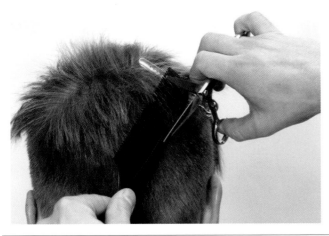

Figure 13.75 Use the scissor over comb technique on the disconnected hair so that the hair lies correctly in the style

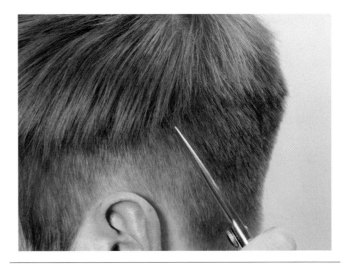

Figure 13.76 Point cut once more to remove any stray bits of hair, using the freehand technique

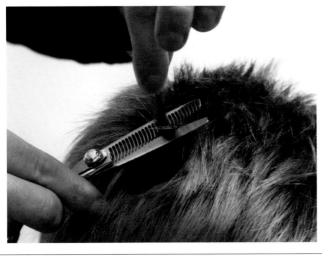

Figure 13.77 In small sections, twist the hair, starting at the bottom. Use thinning scissors to cut. This effect thins and tapers the hair

Figure 13.78 Apply products to the hair to finish the look

Figure 13.79 The finished look

Figure 13.80 The finished look

The finished style incorporated the following techniques and effects:

- club cutting
- clipper over comb
- scissor over comb
- tapering
- freehand
- thinning
- texturising
- graduating.

Creating a layered haircut on curly hair

Figure 13.81 Before the haircut

Figure 13.82 The hair is sectioned into a hot cross bun effect after gowning the client in the appropriate manner

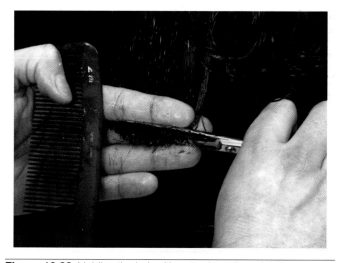

Figure 13.83 Holding the hair with natural tension, club cut to create the baseline

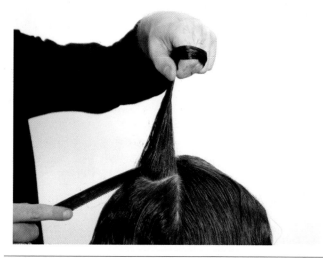

Figure 13.84 Take a rectangle box section on the crown

Figure 13.85 Drop the hair down to see the length the layers should be

Figure 13.86 Club cut to the required length

Figure 13.87 Take the first section from the central profile parting

Figure 13.88 Hold the hair up, twist it round and cut downwards to the guideline. This technique keeps length in the hair. Work down the head in sections

Figure 13.89 Use the razor to create texture and volume to the bottom layers (online video)

Figure 13.90 Use the razor to create texture and volume to the bottom layers (online video)

Figure 13.91 Blow-dry the hair and apply products to finish

Figure 13.92 Finished look

Figure 13.93 Finished look

The finished style incorporated the following techniques and effects:

- club cutting
- tapering
- thinning
- texturising
- layering.

Client care

After cutting, remove any loose clippings of hair from the client's face, neck and shoulders. Make sure that you are happy with the cut you have created and check the balance of the style. Check with the client that he is happy with the finished look. Hold a back mirror up to help the client see the back profile.

Figure 13.94 Remove loose hair from the client's face

13.3 Provide aftercare advice

An important part of this service is to give the client aftercare advice. You should explain to the client how often they should return to the salon to maintain their haircut. This will depend on the length of the client's hair. Clients with shorter styles will need to return to the salon for a trim more often than clients with longer styles. A client's lifestyle must be taken into consideration when creating a style that they can maintain.

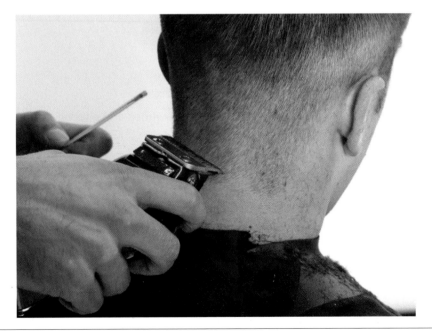

Figure 13.95 This type of style will need regular maintenance

WWW Online activity 13.6

Round the board

Equipment and products

As you are working, always explain to the client how best to use the equipment. They may want to recreate the style themselves at home. Advise the client which products can be used at home. This should be based on the factors that influence the service. Refer to Chapter 4 for more information.

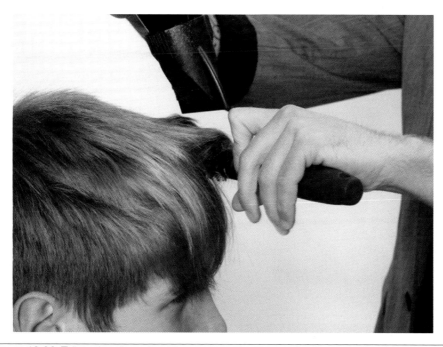

Figure 13.96 Talk to the client about the equipment you are using to create the style

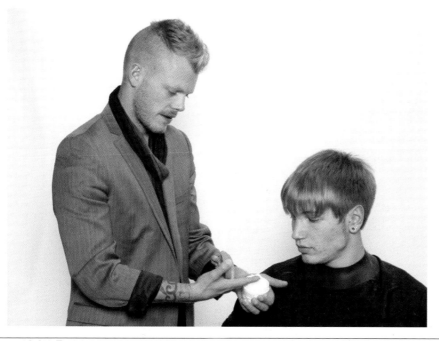

Figure 13.97 Explain to the client which products can be used at home

13.4 Worksheets

You can carry out these worksheets during your study of a chapter or unit, or at the end. An example is presented here and there are more online. Write your answers directly in the book, but only if you own it of course – if it is a library or college book, use a separate piece of paper!

13.4.1 Cutting techniques

Label each of these photos to say which cutting technique is shown and suggest when this would be used.

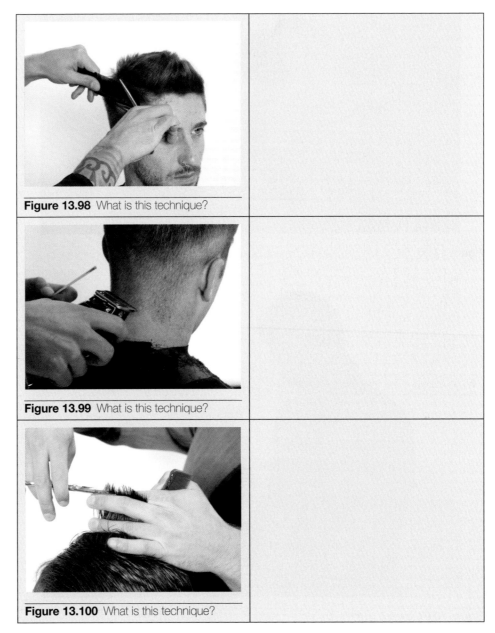

Figure 13.98 What is this technique?

Figure 13.99 What is this technique?

Figure 13.100 What is this technique?

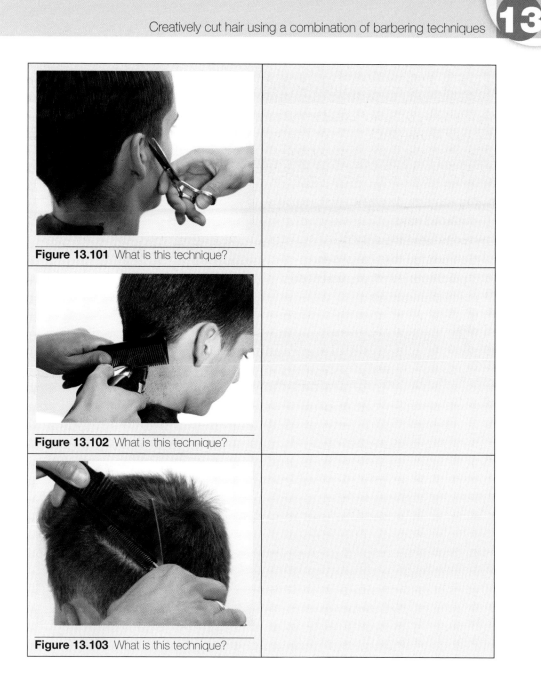

Figure 13.101 What is this technique?

Figure 13.102 What is this technique?

Figure 13.103 What is this technique?

13.5 Assessment

Well done! If you have studied all the content of this unit you may be ready to test your knowledge.

Check out the 'Preparing for assessments' section in Chapter 1 if you have not already done so, and always remember:

- You can only do your best if you have. . .
  - studied hard
  - completed the activities
  - completed the worksheets
  - practised, practised, practised
  - and then revised!

? Now carry out the online multiple-choice quiz

. . . and good luck in the final exam, which will be arranged by your tutor/assessor.

Top tips

Consultation services

Everyone can be trained to become a qualified hairdresser, but those who correctly take the time and care over a client consultation will be amongst the elite.
Kim Gerrish, Hairdressing Program Leader, Wiltshire College, Trowbridge

When advising and consulting with clients, remember that you are the expert and the client is not only paying for a treatment, but for your knowledge and expertise as well!
Samantha Raybould, Yale College, Wrexham

Promote products and services

Don't forget to always make product recommendations throughout the treatment. If you don't, you are doing your client a disservice and they will most definitely spend their money elsewhere, on products that they more than likely don't need.
Samantha Raybould, Yale College, Wrexham

Creatively cut hair

When cutting long hair, don't be afraid to ask the client to stand up and hold on to the back of the chair. This way, you know your client is maintaining correct posture and you can sit on a stool and cut the hair at eye level, therefore ensuring that the cut is accurate.
Lindsay Bellis, Lecturer in Hairdressing and Bridal Hair at Yale College

Never cut hair unless you can see your guideline. This way your haircut should always be balanced.
Lindsay Bellis, Lecturer in Hairdressing and Bridal Hair at Yale College

Colour hair

Use a variety of colours and techniques on clients to give them a bespoke colour. This will make clients loyal to you.
Mandy Durkin, Saks Education

If you're afraid of your foils bleeding, fold up a piece of foil longways until it is approximately one inch thick and wrap it around the top of your packet to prevent it from seeping.
Lindsay Bellis, Lecturer in Hairdressing and Bridal Hair at Yale College

Colour correction

You can never be 100% sure what a client has previously used on their hair. Before agreeing to the service always test a strand of hair with the products needed to correct it in order to ensure that they are compatible.
Carly Embling-Loxton, Helen Ward and Linda Powell, Swindon College

Creatively style and dress hair

When curling hair, work from the nape upwards. Once you have curled a section, pin the curl together like a loose pin curl, with a double pronged silver clip. This will allow the hair to cool in shape and help the curl last longer.
Lindsay Bellis, Lecturer in Hairdressing and Bridal Hair at Yale College

Creatively dress long hair

When putting grips in to secure hair they don't have to be open (often tricky and tempting to use teeth!), just place the bottom of the grip under the strand to be

secured and lift slightly when pushing the grip in. The grip will open slightly with the pressure of the hair.
June Phillips, Lecturer, Hairdressing and Functional Skills, South Devon College

Before you begin your service always check to see what kind of top your client is wearing – if they have to pull it over their head when they take it off it might disrupt the hairstyle!
Carly Embling-Loxton, Helen Ward and Linda Powell, Swindon College

Develop creative skills

Never assume that you have learnt all there is to learn in hairdressing. The best hairdressers are the ones that will say 'I want to learn how to do that'.
Carly Embling-Loxton, Helen Ward and Linda Powell, Swindon College

Design and create facial hair shapes

Encourage your client to exfoliate and soften the skin to reduce ingrowing hairs.
Dawn Buttle, Academy Manager, Salon Services, Hairdressing, South Essex College of Further and Higher Education

Cut creatively using barbering techniques

Apply a moisturiser to your skin before shaving to prevent razor burns.
Breidge Johnston, North West Regional College

Always look in the mirror throughout your haircut to check weight and balance.
Carly Embling-Loxton, Helen Ward and Linda Powell, Swindon College

Glossary

This glossary is also available online at www.atthairdressing.com where you can search for important words and phrases and even translate them into other languages.

We have added a guide to the pronunciation of unusual words in this format: (proh-nun-see-ay-shun), at the front of the book.

Abrasion	*An area of the skin which has worn away.*
Absorbed	*Taken in through the surface of an object.*
Accessories	*Jewellery or other items worn in the hair.*
Accident	*A mishap that can often lead to injury.*
Account	*A record of financial transactions.*
Accuracy	*How close the data given is to the true value.*
Accurate	*Exact.*
Acetic acid	*Used in acid rinses (vinegar rinse).*
Acid	*A solution with a pH of less than 7.*
Acid balanced	*Lotion with the same pH as the skin (4.5-5.5).*
Action plan	*A method of outlining steps and actions in order achieve a particular goal.*
Adapt	*To suit another purpose.*
Added hair	*Extensions and hair pieces.*
Additional media	*Materials other than ornamentation used for creating a look, e.g. accessories, make-up and clothes.*
Additive	*Substance added to improve a product.*
Adequate	*Sufficient.*
Adhere	*To stick to.*
Adhesions	*Scar tissue.*
Advertising	*Promoting product or services.*
Advice	*Guidance offered by someone.*
Afro	*Type of hair.*
Afro comb	*Comb to detangle afro or curly hair.*
Aftercare	*Continuing service given to the client.*
Agitation	*To keep a substance or object moving.*
Alcohol	*Solvent used in setting lotions.*
Alcoholics Anonymous	*A worldwide group of men and women who meet in order to help one another stop drinking alcohol and remain sober.*
Alkaline	*Solution with a pH above 7.*
Allergic reaction	*Abnormal reaction to a substance.*
Allergy	*Abnormal reaction to a substance.*
Almond oil	*Vegetable oil used for hot oil scalp treatments. Ingredient of control creams.*
Alopecia	*A general term meaning baldness.*
Alopecia areata	*Balding condition made up of small round patches which often follow the line of a nerve.*
Alpha keratin	*Hair in its natural unstretched state.*

Alphabetical	*In the order of the letters of the alphabet.*
Alter	*To change.*
Alternative	*A choice.*
Amino acid	*The component units of protein.*
Ammonia	*Colourless fluid used as a solvent.*
Anagen	*During the period of active growth the hair is said to be in anagen.*
Analyse	*Examine in detail, e.g. the condition of the hair.*
Androgenic alopecia	*Hereditary male pattern baldness.*
Annual	*Yearly.*
Annual income	*Amount of money you earn each year.*
Anonymous	*To be unknown.*
Antiseptic	*A substance which prevents the multiplication of germs but does not necessarily kill them. Examples are cetrimide and chloroxylenol.*
Antivirus software	*A software package that prevents computer viruses from damaging or destroying the system.*
Appeal	*To ask urgently.*
Appearance	*The way that somebody looks.*
Application	*Another name for a computer program such as Microsoft Word.*
Appointment	*A specified time for a meeting.*
Appraisal	*A system of reviewing an employee's job performance carried out by the employee and employer.*
Area	*Length x width.*
Artificial	*To be man-made.*
Assemble	*To gather together.*
Assess	*To judge the condition (of hair).*
Assessor	*The candidate's teacher or tutor, who assesses the portfolio of evidence.*
Assistance	*Help.*
Asymmetric	*Unbalanced profile.*
Attract	*To draw an object or substance closer.*
Authorisation	*Agreed by the supervisor.*
Autoclave	*Apparatus used for sterilising tools. It works on the same principle as a pressure cooker.*
Avant-garde	*A term used to describe artwork that breaks away from tradition.*
Average	*The sum divided by the number of items.*
Awarding body	*There are several awarding bodies, for example City and Guilds, AQA, Edexcel and OCR.*
Backbrushing	*Achieves a soft effect and will 'fluff' the hair with more bounce.*
Backcombing	*Achieves a stiff style.*
Backup	*A second copy of work in case the original is damaged or destroyed. Should be stored away from the computer.*
Backwash	*Flow of water directed backwards.*
Bacteria	*Disease causing micro-organisms.*
Balance	*Equal distribution.*
Bands of colour	*Areas of the hair that appear lighter or darker than the rest of the hair.*
Barbicide	*Chemical used to sterilise tools.*
Barrel curl	*Used on very short hair to achieve the same result as rollers.*
Barrier	*Something that blocks things from going past it.*

Barrier cream	*A cream used to protect skin from contact with products.*
Base colour	*The client's natural hair colour.*
Baseline	*Lowest point and foundation of haircut.*
Basic skills	*Reading, writing, speaking in English (or Welsh) and using numbers sufficiently well to be able to function in society and at work. Key skills and basic skills overlap at Levels 1 and 2.*
Basin	*A sink. Used to wash clients' hair.*
Beta keratin	*The stretched (wet) state of hair.*
Biased	*Favouring one thing over another.*
Bicarbonate	*Mineral of hard water.*
Binds	*Ties to.*
Bleach	*Chemical used to lighten (whiten) hair colour by oxidisation.*
Blending	*Combining two sections.*
Block colouring technique	*Colouring the hair in a large area.*
Blow-drying	*The method of drying the hair using a hand dryer.*
Bluetooth	*Wireless technology. A chip is responsible for the transmission of data between a wide range of devices (mobile phone and hands-free system) through short range digital two-way radio.*
Bob	*A one-length haircut.*
Body language	*Refers to facial expressions, gestures or a particular way a person is standing. Non-verbal communication.*
Brick cutting	*A technique of texturising by cutting small parts of hair in a 'brick' fashion.*
Brickwork	*Term used for positioning rollers correctly.*
Brittle	*Hair that can be easily broken.*
Buckled	*To be out of shape.*
Budget	*A list of incomings and outgoings used in financial planning.*
Burdock root oil	*Used in shampoos for dry scalp.*
Calcium	*Mineral affecting the hardness of water.*
Canities	*Pigmentation cells not functioning; hair turns white.*
Capability	*The ability to complete a task.*
Cape	*Waterproof gown used to protect a client's clothes.*
Capillary	*Very thin blood vessel.*
Career prospect	*The direction in which your career could move.*
Cash	*Money, banknotes and coins.*
Catagen	*Stage of hair growth: hair falls out, follicle shrinks.*
CD ROM	*Compact Disk Read Only Memory. Stores up to 800 Mb of data. The data is 'read only' which means that you cannot change or overwrite it.*
Ceramic	*An object that is made into a shape and then hardened using heat.*
Cetrimide	*Antiseptic chemical used for pityriasis capitis.*
Characteristic	*A feature or quality of a person, place or thing.*
Checking	*Hair has a balanced front, sides, sections match.*
Cheque	*Written order to bank for payment.*
Cheque guarantee card	*Guarantee by bank for payment of the order.*
Chip and PIN	*Customers key in a PIN at point of sale instead of signing a receipt.*
Chlorinated water	*Water with added chlorine; can damage the hair.*
Cicatricial alopecia	*Baldness caused by physical/chemical damage to skin.*
Circular brush	*Used to loosen out the set or achieve a softer look.*

Circumference	*The boundary line of a circle.*
Clarify	*To make clear.*
Clarifying	*To make clear.*
Classic	*A look that will not age.*
Client suggestion box	*A box used by clients to post written feedback.*
Climazone	*Equipment to dry hair and speed chemical processes.*
Clipboard	*A temporary area used to store copied information.*
Clipper over comb	*Technique for cutting hair. Clippers are used to cut hair following the movement over a comb.*
Clock-spring curls	*Tight curls or wave movements.*
Clockwise	*To move in the same direction as the hands on a clock.*
Closed question	*A question with a definite answer e.g. yes/no.*
Club cutting	*Hair cut straight across.*
Coal tar	*Chemical with antiseptic qualities.*
Coarse hair	*Hair with thick shaft.*
Coconut	*Used in shampoos for dry scalps.*
Colleagues	*The people you work with.*
Collodion	*A syrupy, clean solution of pyroxylin, alcohol and ether.*
Colour correction	*The way in which hair colour or bleach problems is corrected.*
Colour reducer	*A product used to remove permanent hair colour.*
Colour reduction	*Removal of permanent colour from the hair.*
Colour star	*Colour chart to achieve desired colour.*
Colour test	*Test used to monitor colour development.*
Colour tone	*Warm/cool shades of colour tints.*
Commitment	*To bind yourself to a certain action.*
Communicate	*To exchange information.*
Communication	*An exchange of thoughts and information.*
Complementary skills	*Skills other than hairdressing but nonetheless essential.*
Comprehensive	*To cover a wide area.*
Compulsory	*Must be completed.*
Computer application	*Programs such as Word, Excel and PowerPoint.*
Computer crash	*An event that causes the computer to become inactive. This can often result in the loss of unsaved work.*
Computerised	*Performed by using a computer.*
Concave	*To curve inwards.*
Concentrated	*A liquid that has had its dilution reduced.*
Concise	*Expressing a lot but in few words.*
Condition	*Reference to the state of the hair's health.*
Conditioner	*Product used to enhance hair condition.*
Confidence	*A feeling of trust.*
Confidential information	*Information that is private and should be protected.*
Confidentiality	*To keep secret.*
Confirm	*To make more firm by repeating.*
Constricted	*Made smaller than normal.*
Constructive	*To improve.*
Consultation	*Discuss with the client individual needs.*
Contagious	*Infection can be transferred by contact.*

Contamination	*Spread of disease by contact of non-sterile objects.*
Contradictory	*To oppose in disagreement.*
Contraindication	*A condition preventing a treatment.*
Contribution	*To give.*
Conventional	*Ordinary.*
Conversion factor	*Used to make it easier when converting from one form of 'measurement' to another.*
Conversions	*To change one expression to another. For example, expressing miles in kilometres.*
Convex	*To curve outwards.*
Cool shade	*Colours such as blue.*
Co-operative	*To join in and help others in your team.*
Cornrows	*Braids that are plaited close to the scalp.*
Cortex	*Middle layer of the hair shaft.*
Courteous	*To be polite.*
Cowlick	*A growth pattern of the hair.*
Creative	*To be artistic.*
Credit	*System of allowing customers to pay later for services.*
Creeping oxidation	*Active product left on the hair separating the cuticle plates.*
Crimping iron	*Tool used for crimping the hair.*
Crocodile clamps	*Used to hold hair while sectioning.*
Cross-check	*Checking haircut.*
Cross-infection	*The spreading of infection between individuals and objects.*
Cross-section	*The area exposed if a cut were to be made through the centre of an object.*
Crown	*The top of the head.*
Crucial	*Very important.*
Curl rearranger	*The product used in the first step of a two-step perm.*
Curling	*To form curls in the hair.*
Curling tongs	*Used for curling the hair.*
Currency	*A unit of exchange used as a form of money.*
Current	*A look that is fashionable.*
Cut-throat razor	*Used for tapering wet hair and shaving.*
Cuticle	*Outer layer of the hair shaft.*
Cysteine	*An amino acid joined by sulphur bonds.*
Damaged cuticle	*Cuticle scale open, absorbs moisture.*
Data Protection Act	*An Act that provides rights for individuals regarding the obtaining, use, holding and disclosure of information about themselves.*
Debit	*Cash deducted from a customer's account.*
Debit card	*A card guarantee that a debit will be honoured by the bank.*
Decimal	*A number system that uses a base of 10.*
Decimal place	*The position of numbers after (to the right of) the decimal point.*
Decomposition	*The breakdown of a material.*
Defamatory	*Untrue and harmful information.*
Denman brush	*A type of brush used for achieving a thorough brush.*
Dense	*Thick.*
Depth	*The natural lightness/darkness of the hair.*

Dermal papilla	*Situated at the hair follicle base, supplying all the materials needed for growth.*
Dermatitis	*Abnormal skin condition.*
Dermis	*Lower layer of the skin.*
Design	*The arrangement of elements.*
Design plan	*A document used for planning a project outlining objectives, budget, roles and responsibilities, resources, health and safety issue etc.*
Designated	*To have been selected for a task or duty.*
Detergent	*Cleaning substance used in shampoos.*
Determine	*To decide.*
Dexterity	*To perform tasks with the hands, using skill.*
Diagnose	*Identify the problem, need or want.*
Diameter	*The line that goes through the centre of the circle.*
Dictionary	*A book containing a list of words in alphabetical order. Each word has information given about it (e.g. the definition).*
Diet	*Nutrient content and food calorific value.*
Diffuse alopecia	*Condition in which the hair thins gradually.*
Diffuser	*Attachment to a dryer for special effect.*
Digit	*A number.*
Dilute	*Weaken the concentration (strength) of a solution.*
Disconnected	*A type of haircut featuring different lengths without being blended together.*
Discriminatory	*Unfair or unequal treatment of a person due to their age, sex, disability, race, religion etc.*
Disk drives	*The primary data storage device used by computers. It stores and retrieves data.*
Dispense	*To give out.*
Disposable	*Designed to be thrown away after use.*
Dissatisfied	*Not happy.*
Distribute	*Spread out.*
Distributed	*Spread out.*
Di-sulphide bond	*Sulphur link of two cystine amino acids.*
Dizziness	*A spinning sensation.*
Double baseline	*Working (cutting) on an extra line over a shorter one.*
Double booking	*Two treatments scheduled at the same time.*
Double crown	*A growth pattern where the crowns jump and swirl in opposite directions.*
Dressing hair	*The way in which hair is finished using different techniques, e.g. smoothing or curling.*
Dressing out	*Styling hair.*
Dressing out brush	*Brush that has a rubber base for more gentle brushing.*
Droop	*To sag, or hang loosely.*
Dry setting	*Hair is altered temporarily using heated rollers.*
Dryer	*Equipment for drying hair; can be hand held or floor standing.*
Duty	*Something that you are obliged to do.*
Effect	*The consequence of.*
Effective	*To work well.*
Efficient	*To get the job done with little waste of time or energy.*
Effleurage	*Smooth stroking massage movement, using palm of the hand.*
EFTPOS	*Electronic Point of Sale.*
Elasticity test	*Test used to assess damage to cortex of hair.*

Eliminate	*To remove.*
Email	*Electronic mail. Messages sent from one person to another electronically via a computer.*
Emergency services	*Fire, Ambulance, Police.*
Emerging	*A look that is nearly in fashion.*
Emoticons	*A way of expressing emotions in online communication, e.g., :-).*
Emotion	*State of feeling, associated with stress, which can affect the condition of the hair.*
Empathise	*To understand someone else's feelings.*
Emulsify	*To blend two liquids that wouldn't naturally combine together.*
Emulsifying agent	*Chemical that blends two liquids that wouldn't naturally combine together.*
Emulsion	*A mixture of two or more liquids that do not blend together.*
Emulsion bleach	*Type of bleach used for full head treatment.*
Enhance	*To make the best of.*
Enquiry	*A question.*
Ensure	*To make certain.*
Epidermis	*Outer layer of the skin.*
Equal opportunities	*Everyone to be given equal rights.*
Equipment	*An instrument.*
Establish	*To find out.*
Estimate	*To guess, but based on experience!*
Ethical	*Morally correct.*
Eumelanin	*Black and brown pigments.*
Evacuate	*To remove.*
Evaluate	*To assess.*
Evidence	*This is what a candidates needs to produce to prove they have the skills required.*
Exaggerate	*To emphasise.*
Exerting	*To use or apply.*
Exhibition	*An event at which products and services are advertised and sold.*
Expire	*To finish.*
Expression	*A way to communicate.*
Extension	*An additional set of numbers that connects to the same telephone line.*
External assessment	*A test set externally to check portfolio evidence.*
Extinguish	*To put out.*
Fatigue	*Tiredness: can be caused by poor working posture.*
Faulty	*Does not work.*
Feasible	*To be capable of being achieved.*
Feathering	*Technique used to remove volume or length of hair.*
Feature	*A characteristic of a person's face.*
Feedback	*The opinions of others or yourself concerned with a product or service.*
Filing system	*Method of keeping records of client treatments.*
Financial	*Monetary.*
Fine hair	*Term used to describe thin or delicate hair strands.*
Fine pins	*Equipment used to secure pin curls or dress hair up.*
Finger drying	*To dry hair using a hairdryer and your hands.*
Finger waving	*Technique where hair is moulded into an 'S' shape using fingers and comb. Also known as water waving.*
Finishing spray	*A product that holds hair in place and protects against weather and humidity.*

Fire extinguisher	*A device for putting out small fires.*
Fixing	*Alternative name for neutralising hair.*
Flamboyant	*To be excessively ornamented.*
Flammable	*Can catch fire.*
Flat brush	*A brush used for smoothing the hair. Also known as spiral brush.*
Flexible	*Being able to accept change.*
Floppy disk	*A portable disk that stores 1.44 Mb of information.*
Focused	*To the point.*
Foils	*Thin sheets of metal generally used for highlighting/lowlighting hair.*
Follicle	*Sac containing the hair shaft in the epidermis.*
Folliculitis	*Bacterial infection of the follicle.*
Forgery	*A copy that is illegal.*
Fractions	*A number of parts out of another number of parts.*
Fragilitas crinium	*Hair splits at the ends and along the shaft.*
Fraud	*The act of deceiving to obtain money.*
Freehand cutting	*Cutting without tension.*
Friction massage	*Used during shampooing to work from the front of the scalp to the nape using the pads of the fingers in a vigorous movement.*
Fungi	*Parasitic organisms that do not contain chlorophyll. Includes mushrooms and yeast.*
Gel	*Lotion used to make hair spiky or stand up.*
General practitioner	*A doctor.*
Gesture	*A hand or body motion.*
Glare	*Reflection from the sun or a light onto the computer screen making it difficult to see properly.*
Gloss	*Lotion used to make hair look shiny.*
Goals	*Objectives relating to a particular time. Can be short-term or long-term.*
Google	*Popular search engine.*
Gown	*Protective garment used to cover clients' clothes.*
Gradient	*The degree of incline.*
Graduation	*The shape of a style created by cutting hair to achieve a look where the inner length is longer than the outer length.*
Grammar	*Forming well written, easy to read sentences, paragraphs and documents with the use of punctuation (full stops, commas etc.).*
Grievance	*To have felt grief after a wrongdoing has occurred. A formal complaint.*
Growth pattern	*The direction of the hair growth.*
Guideline	*Mesh of hair used to measure other sections.*
Hair balance	*Profile shape of the hairstyle.*
Hair extensions	*Additional pieces of hair attached to current hair.*
Hair shaft	*The part of the hair that is above the skin.*
Hair straighteners	*Heated styling equipment designed to straighten the hair. Can also be used for other styling techniques.*
Hair structure	*The microscopic make-up of hair.*
Hairline	*Natural hairline around the neck and face.*
Hairspray	*A product that holds hair in place and protects against weather and humidity.*
Hard disk	*A storage device that holds large amounts of data.*
Hard water	*Water with increased levels of calcium; requires more soap and detergent; forms scum.*

Hardware	*The physical components of a computer system.*
Hazard	*A source of danger.*
Hazardous	*Involving risk or danger.*
Heart shape	*Face shape for which suitable hairstyles include a fringe and hair between ear and jaw.*
Heat protectors	*Products applied to prevent the hair becoming damaged from heated styling equipment.*
Heated rollers	*Creates volume root lift, curl and hair direction.*
Heated tongs	*An electrical device used to curl hair.*
Henna	*Permanent vegetable tint.*
Hereditary	*Passed on from parents (genetic).*
Herpes simplex	*A viral infection affecting the skin and nervous system.*
Hexachlorophene	*Chemical used with antiseptic properties used on dry scalp.*
Hierarchy	*A group of people ranked in order of job position.*
Highlights	*Lightening strands of hair.*
Hinder	*To prevent something.*
Hologram	*A 3-D image.*
Hood dryer	*Floor mounted dryer; creates an overall even drying effect quickly.*
Hormone	*Chemical produced by the body controlling chemical reactions in the body.*
Hospitality	*The way in which a client is welcomed and received into the salon.*
Hostility	*Unfriendly.*
Humidity	*The dampness in the air.*
Hydrogen	*Flammable gas occurring in water and ammonia.*
Hydrogen bond	*A chemical bonding linking oxygen to hydrogen to form water.*
Hydrogen peroxide	*An agent used for oxidising when colouring and perming.*
Hydrophilic	*Will mix with water.*
Hydrophobic	*Will not mix with water (repelled).*
Hygiene	*Principles and practice of sanitation to ensure good health.*
Hygroscopic	*Absorbs moisture.*
ICT	*Information and communication technology.*
Identify	*To consider.*
Image	*A perception of (hair salon's image).*
Immiscible	*Liquids that are incapable of mixing together.*
Imperial measurements	*Defined by three measures – the gallon, the yard and the pound.*
Impetigo	*Contagious bacterial skin disease.*
Impression	*Outward appearance.*
Incapacitated	*A person with a mental, emotional or physical impairment.*
Incoming telephone call	*To receive a telephone call.*
Incompatibility test	*Method of detecting products used in previous treatments that may counter-react.*
Incompatible	*Cannot be used with (other chemicals).*
Incorporating	*To include.*
Infection	*A disease caused by micro-organisms.*
Infectious	*The spreading of disease.*
Infestation	*A group of parasites.*
Infirm	*(A person) lacking in strength.*
Inflation	*The general increase in the price of goods and services.*

Ingest	*Take into the body by the mouth.*
Ingredient	*Part of.*
Inhalation	*Take into the body through the airways.*
Initial and diagnostic assessment	*This is carried out to find a candidate's strengths and weaknesses, current levels of attainment and potential.*
Initiative	*To take the first step.*
Innovative	*To be forward thinking in terms of ideas and themes.*
Input device	*A device that allows you to put information into the computer, e.g. keyboard, mouse.*
Interactive	*Two-way communication.*
Internal	*Inside.*
Internal shape	*Internal shape of the haircut.*
Internal verification	*The process whereby a centre ensures it operates consistently and to national standards in interpreting and assessing the key skills.*
Internet	*A worldwide network of computers that allows us to view the World Wide Web.*
Interpersonal skills	*The ability to deal well with several different people.*
Interpret	*To understand and be able to explain something.*
Interpreted	*To make sense of.*
Inter-quartile mean	*The average of the values in the inter-quartile range.*
Inter-quartile range	*The range of numbers with the upper and lower quartiles removed.*
Intertwining	*To twist together.*
Intimidating	*To make somebody feel uncomfortable, timid or even fearful.*
Inversion	*Create a concave shape in the hair.*
Inward nape	*Nape hair grows strongly to the centre.*
Irritant	*A chemical that can cause irritation or inflammation of the skin.*
Irritate	*To annoy or cause discomfort.*
IT	*Information technology.*
Itemise	*To list individually.*
Job description	*A set of responsibilities given by an employer for a particular job.*
Journal	*Day by day diary or similar.*
Keloid	*Irregular fibrous tissue which is formed at the place of a scar or injury.*
Keratin	*Protein that makes up hair. Contains large amounts of sulphur.*
Key data	*Important, relevant information.*
Keyboard	*The typewriter-like keys used to input data into a computer. An input device.*
Knowledge	*To know something.*
Lanolin	*Product used in shampoos used for a dry scalp.*
Lanugo	*Foetal body hair.*
Latent heat	*Body heat from the scalp.*
Layering	*Hair cut at various angles.*
Legislation	*A law.*
Libellous	*Untrue and harmful information.*
Library	*Collection of materials, e.g. books or CDs.*
Lice	*Fleas, insects that infest the hair.*
Lift	*Lightening the hair colour.*
Lightening	*To remove colour from the hair.*
Limescale	*Deposit of bicarbonates caused by boiling water.*
Long shape	*Face shape suited by fuller sides hairstyle and flatter on top.*

Lotion	*Product that has the consistency of a light cream.*
Lower quartile	*Data is split into 4 equal quarters. The lowest quarter is referred to as the lower quartile. For example the lower quartile of 100 is the lowest 25 of the numbers.*
Lowlights	*Sections of hair that have been toned darker than the full head of hair.*
Magnesium	*Mineral affecting the hardness of the water.*
Maintain	*To keep something at a specific level.*
Maintenance	*To care for.*
Manoeuvre	*To move.*
Manual	*Not computerised.*
Mapping	*Used to identify opportunities for developing and assessing key skills within the curriculum.*
Marcel iron	*Equipment used for setting hair.*
Marketing	*The method of advertising, promoting and selling to customers.*
Massage	*Manipulative movement using the fingers and palms of the hand.*
MasterCard	*Type of credit card.*
Mb	*Megabyte. Used to measure computer memory. 1 Mb = 1,000,000 bytes or 1024 Kb (kilobytes).*
Mean	*The average value (the sum divided by the number of items).*
Median	*The middle number of a series when the data is arranged in ascending order.*
Medicated	*Contains healing or medical additives.*
Medium hair	*Hair shaft is middle-range in size.*
Medulla	*The central part of the hair shaft.*
Melanin	*Colouring pigment of the hair.*
Melanocytes	*A cell that contains the pigment melanin.*
Memory chip	*A chip that stores data.*
Merchandise	*Goods that are to be sold.*
Merely	*No more than.*
Meshes	*Smaller sections of main sections.*
Method	*The way in which a task is carried out.*
Methodically	*To work through something in the correct order.*
Metric measurement	*A system designed to regulate measurement. Each quantity has a single unit. These include metre, kilogram, ampere.*
Micro-organisms	*Tiny forms of life, only seen through a microscope.*
Microphone	*A device that converts sound waves to audio signals.*
Microsoft Office	*A package of programs including Word Processor (Word), Spreadsheet (Excel), Presentation (PowerPoint), Email and Organisation (Outlook).*
Misconception	*To have the wrong impression.*
Mobility	*Movement.*
Mode	*The most common number in a series.*
Modifications	*Changes made.*
Moisturise	*Add or restore moisture to the hair.*
Molecule	*Chemical unit of two or more atoms.*
Monilethrix	*Uneven production of cells in dermal papilla causing brittle hair.*
Monitor	*The screen that displays information produced on a computer. An output device.*
Moulding	*To sculpture the hair.*
Mouse	*An input device that allows the user to move the pointer around the screen and click on different items to operate computer applications.*

Mousse foam	*Lotion used for setting hair.*
Multiple-choice	*A selection of answers.*
Nape	*Lowest point of hair growth at the back of the head.*
Natural base	*Natural colour of the hair.*
Natural parting	*A natural parting where the hair falls making a dividing line.*
Navigation	*The way in which you get around a program or website.*
Negative communication	*A comment or statement expressing lack of approval.*
Negative ions	*Electrically charged atoms.*
Network	*Interlinked group of computers so that resources can be shared.*
Network card	*A piece of hardware that allows computers to be connected to a network.*
Neutralise	*Fixing the structure of the hair after permanent waving or relaxing.*
Nitro-dyes	*Semi-permanent colouring dyes.*
Non-contagious	*Infection that cannot be transferred by contact.*
Non-verbal	*Any form of communication that does not use words, e.g. traffic lights, shaking somebody's hand and smiling.*
Normalising	*Alternative word for neutralising.*
Nozzle	*Attachment for dryer to achieve a special effect.*
Objective information	*Information that is unbiased and open minded.*
Objectives	*The goals to be achieved.*
Obligatory	*Compulsory.*
Obscene	*Offensive, foul, disgusting.*
Obstacles	*Objects that are in the way.*
Occipital bone	*Convex protruding bone at the back of the skull.*
Occupation	*The job that you do. For example, training to be a motor mechanic is training for an occupation.*
Odour	*Smell or fragrance.*
Offensive	*To attack somebody/something by words or physically.*
Office applications	*A package of programs including Word Processor (Word), Spreadsheet (Excel), Presentation (PowerPoint), Email and Organisation (Outlook).*
One-length cut	*Hair cut in a 'bob'.*
Open-centred pin curls	*Loose, soft pin curls.*
Open question	*A question used to allow respondent to expand on their answer.*
Opinion	*A personal belief.*
Organisms	*Life forms made of a complex system of cells and tissues.*
Ornamentation	*Decoration to be added to hair once it has been styled.*
Outgoing telephone call	*To make a telephone call to somebody.*
Output device	*A device that allows information from the computer to be displayed, e.g., monitor, printer.*
Outside shape	*Shape of the hair cut on the baseline.*
Oval shape	*The perfect shaped face to suit any hairstyle.*
Overlap	*Time of a treatment going into the time scheduled for another.*
Oxidation	*The addition of oxygen in a chemical reaction.*
Oxymelanin	*Melanin reduced by bleach.*
Packet	*An item used to colour hair in sections.*
Paddle brush	*Used for smoothing hair.*
Parasite	*An organism that feeds from and lives on another organism.*
Participate	*To take part in.*

Particle	*A tiny part of an object.*
Pear shape	*Face shape for which suitable hairstyles should have lots of volume around the temples but flat around the jaw line.*
Pediculosis capitis	*To be infected with lice on the scalp.*
Penetrate	*To enter.*
Penetrating conditioner	*Work by penetrating the cortex and help to repair damage by adding protein. They are known as substantive products.*
Per cent	*The proportion of one part of something to the whole. Per means 'out of' and 'cent' means 'hundred'.*
Percentage change	*Changed amounts divided by the original value, then multiplied by 100.*
Performance criteria	*The standards from which you (the student) will be evaluated.*
Perimeter	*The sum of all the outside edges of a shape.*
Perm rod	*Rod around which hair is re-shaped.*
Permanent colour	*Colour containing molecules that penetrate the cuticle and are absorbed into the cortex. The tint remains until it is cut out.*
Perming	*The method of curling hair by altering the structure using chemicals.*
Petrissage	*A deep kneading massage movement.*
pH	*Level of acidity/alkalinity.*
Pharmacist	*Somebody who carries out the service of preparing and distributing medicine.*
Pheomelanin	*Natural pigment of hair causing a red/yellow hair colour.*
Phrase	*A group of words in sequence.*
Pi	*3.141592 (3.142) (in mathematics).*
Pigment	*Colour matter of the hair.*
Pin curling	*Open-centre pin curl used to achieve loose flat look.*
Pine	*Product used in shampoos for dry scalp.*
Pityriasis capitis	*Continuous flaking of the epidermis (dandruff).*
Plagiarise	*Taking another person's work as your own.*
Plaiting	*Used to achieve a secure finish after dressing hair out.*
Planning	*The act of forming and following a programme to achieve a specific goal.*
Pleating	*Folds of hair secured with pins and grips.*
Pli	*Hair set in rollers or pin curls.*
Point to root	*Winding the hair from the ends of the hair to the root.*
Pointing	*Technique used to break up the points of the hair.*
Policy	*A plan of action.*
Polite	*To show regard to others. To have good manners.*
Polythene	*Lightweight plastic.*
Ponytail	*A hairstyle where the hair is drawn to the back of the head and secured with a band.*
Population of UK	*Number of people that live in the UK (about 70 million by 2013).*
Porosity	*Ability to absorb moisture.*
Portfolio	*This is usually a folder that contains the evidence chosen to illustrate competence to satisfy individual key skills requirements.*
Positive communication	*A comment or statement expressing approval.*
Positive ions	*Electrically charged atoms.*
Posture	*Working position of the body.*
Potential	*Possibility that something may happen.*
Powder bleach	*Type of bleach used for highlights. Not usually recommended for full head.*

PPE	*Personal protective equipment. Equipment that is worn, protecting people at work from risks to their health and safety.*
Precaution	*A method of reducing risk.*
Precise	*To be exact and accurate.*
Pre-colouring	*Applying a treatment to the hair before colouring to improve the condition.*
Pre-perm shampoo	*Soapless detergent shampoo with no additives.*
Pre-perm test	*Detection of extent of curl from a previous perm.*
Pre-pigmentation	*The method of adding a warm shade to the hair to replace missing pigments before re-colouring bleached hair.*
Presentation	*The way in which something is displayed.*
Pre-softening	*The application of a treatment to lift the cuticle from the hair allowing the colour to penetrate the cortex.*
Pre-wrap lotion	*Method used to even out the porosity of hair.*
Pricing scanner	*A device that converts a visual form into a price.*
Prickly	*Sensation of cut hair next to client's skin.*
Primary colours	*Yellow, blue and red.*
Printer	*An output device that allows data from the computer to be displayed on paper.*
Probationary	*A trial period.*
Procedure	*A course of action.*
Processing time	*The length of time it takes for colour to develop.*
Processor	*The central processing unit oversees all of the other components of the system. Can be thought of as the brain of the computer.*
Product	*Item sold as part of the hair care process.*
Professional	*Term given to use of effective and efficient working methods.*
Profile	*Shape of the hairstyle.*
Profitable	*To obtain positive income from a transaction.*
Progress	*Positive development.*
Promotional	*To advertise or publicise.*
Promptly	*Straight away.*
Proportion	*The size of different parts in relation to each other.*
Props	*Items used for events.*
Protective gloves	*Rubber gloves used to protect hands from chemicals.*
Protective treatment	*Products used to stop damage to hair that has previously been treated. Applied before treatment.*
Protein	*Hair structure, made from amino acids.*
Protrude	*To stick out.*
Provenance	*The origins of information.*
PSI	*Pounds per square inch.*
Psoriasis	*Red patches on scalp covered by silver white scales.*
Pubic	*Type of terminal hair.*
Publicity	*To get attention for a product/service by advertising etc.*
Punctuation	*The use of marks and signs to form words, sentences, paragraphs etc.*
Qualified	*To have the necessary skills and abilities to perform a job.*
Quantify	*To put something into figures.*
Quartile	*Any three points that divide an ordered distribution into four parts. Each of these parts contains a quarter of the score.*

Quasi-permanent	*Non-permanent method of colouring hair. Fades over a longer period than semi-permanent.*
Questionnaire	*A set of questions used for collecting feedback.*
Racist	*Intolerance of race. A person with prejudiced belief that one race is superior to (better than) another.*
Radius	*A line running from the centre of the circle to the circumference.*
Rake comb	*Large toothed comb for wet/tangled hair.*
Range	*The difference between the highest and lowest numbers.*
Rapport	*An agreement of trust between hairdresser and client.*
Rash	*Contraindication response by the body to a chemical.*
Rate of lift	*Lightening of hair colour.*
Ratio	*The comparison of two numbers.*
React	*To respond.*
Reaction	*When chemicals cause a substance to change.*
Rebonding	*Re-fixing amino acids in the neutralising process to re-form cystine.*
Receding	*Gradually moving from the front to the back.*
Reception	*Greeting.*
Recession areas	*Growth pattern – bald areas around the hairline.*
Recognition	*To identify a thing or person.*
Record	*History of client's treatments.*
Record card	*Method of recording client's treatments.*
Rectify	*To set right.*
Referral	*To suggest or recommend.*
Regenerate	*To renew or replace.*
Regime	*A method or plan.*
Regulate	*Adjust (the temperature of the water).*
Regulations	*Rules.*
Reinforce	*To make information sink in. To confirm.*
Relaxing	*The method of reducing a natural curl by altering the structure either temporarily or permanently using chemicals.*
Relevant information	*The suitability of information based upon your needs.*
Repel	*To reject.*
Represent	*Acting on behalf of someone.*
Reputable	*To have a good reputation.*
Research	*To study something thoroughly.*
Resistant	*Not affected by.*
Resolution	*The number of pixels per square inch shown on the computer screen. The greater the resolution the better the picture.*
Resolve	*To correct.*
Resources	*Sources of information, expertise and knowledge.*
Respect	*To think of highly.*
Respond	*To answer to.*
Retail	*To be sold.*
Revenue	*Income.*
Review	*To look over and study information again.*
Revision	*To review information in order to remind yourself of its content.*
Ringworm	*A fungal skin infection.*

Rinse	*Process of cleaning, usually with water.*
RIRO	*Rubbish In Rubbish Out. In relation to the Internet.*
Risk	*The likelihood of an accident occurring from a hazard.*
Risk assessment	*The process of calculating the risk associated with a hazard and the actions taken to avoid it.*
Role	*A set of activities or actions attached to a job.*
Roll	*A hairstyle created by folding the hair and securing with pins.*
Roller	*A cylindrical styling tool used to create waves or curls.*
Root lift	*Creating volume at the root.*
Root movement	*Amount of lift achieve at the hair root.*
Root to point	*Winding the hair from the roots to the ends of the hair.*
Rotary massage	*Second massage movement in shampooing using the pads of the fingers in quick, circular movements.*
Round shape	*Face shaped suited by flat sides, full on top hairstyle.*
Rounding off	*Express as a round number (e.g. 4.7 rounded off becomes 5).*
Routine	*A course of action that is followed every day.*
RSI	*Repetitive strain injury. This type of injury occurs from repeated physical movements. It can be caused by bad typing technique, bad posture and lack of adequate rest and breaks. RSI is common in the wrists.*
Sale	*To sell.*
Satisfied	*To be happy with something.*
Scabies	*Raised red lines on the skin caused by itch mite.*
Scalding	*Burning of the skin (by water that is too hot).*
Scales	*Outer part of the cuticle.*
Scalp	*Skin of the top of the head.*
Scalp protector	*Product applied to hairline and scalp to protect against chemicals in products.*
Scanning	*To skim/scan text in order to get a general idea about it.*
Schedule	*To plan a time and place.*
Scissor over comb	*A cutting technique. Scissors are used to cut hair rapidly following the movement over a comb.*
Scrunch drying	*A technique of drying the hair using a diffuser to enhance curls or waves.*
Scum	*Calcium stearate formed from soap and mineral salts in hard water.*
Sea	*Salty water (e.g. sea water) causes damage to hair.*
Search engine	*A program that enables you to locate information on the World Wide Web using keyword searches.*
Sebaceous cyst	*Lump on scalp caused by blocked sebaceous gland.*
Sebaceous gland	*Produces sebum.*
Seborrhoea	*Condition in which excess sebum is produced by the sebaceous glands.*
Sebum	*Oily secretion from the sebaceous glands.*
Secondary colours	*Colours made from mixing primary shades together. Orange, green and violet.*
Section	*Main divisions when dividing the hair for a particular hairdressing service.*
Section clips	*Used for sectioning hair.*
Seminar	*A conference or meeting to discuss a certain subject.*
Semi-permanent	*Type of colour group (nitro-dyes).*
Semi-permanent colour	*Colour molecules deposited in the hair cuticle or under the open cuticle. They will lighten each time the hair is shampooed.*
Sequence	*One thing that follows on to the next.*

Serum	*Product applied during styling to give the hair shine.*
Services	*Alternative name for hair treatment.*
Sesame	*Product used in shampoos for dry scalp.*
Setting comb	*A comb used for finger waving or dressing hair.*
Setting hair	*Setting hair into range of styles and effects.*
Setting mousse	*A product that is applied to wet hair in order to keep style in place.*
Setting pins	*Used for securing rollers in place.*
Shade chart	*Method of identifying the target shade.*
Shadowing	*Following a more experienced member of staff for training purposes.*
Shampoo	*Detergent to wash or clean hair.*
Shine	*Spray lotion applied to hair to achieve a shiny finish.*
Significant figures	*The number of digits expressed in a measurement. Sig. fig. can appear before and/ or after the decimal point.*
Signposting guidance	*Within the specifications for the new AS levels, A levels and GNVQs, opportunities for developing or producing evidence for assessment of key skills.*
Simulations	*Activities that simulate or model reality.*
Sincere	*To be genuine.*
Skim-reading	*To skim/scan text in order to get a general idea about it.*
Skin test	*Application of the product to the skin to assess the reaction.*
Slice colouring technique	*Colouring small sections of hair.*
Slide cutting	*Scissors are slipped through the hair to achieve tapering (feathering) effect.*
Sodium hydroxide	*Lye contained in relaxers.*
Soft water	*Reduced level of mineral content. Water suds easily.*
Software	*A computer program.*
Sparingly	*To use a small amount.*
Sparse	*Not dense. Thin.*
Speakers	*Device that converts audio signals to sounds that humans can hear.*
Specialise	*To devote yourself to a particular area of work.*
Spell checker	*Most computer applications (e.g. Microsoft Word, Excel etc.) will enable you to check documents for incorrect spelling.*
Spelling	*To form a word with a series of letters.*
Spider diagrams	*A series of lines and boxes containing relevant information. A form of note taking.*
Spiral	*Type of setting technique. Also a type of brush known as a circular brush.*
Spot colouring	*Applying colour to certain parts of the hair that need it.*
Spreadsheet	*A computer program often used to create financial forecasting documents.*
Square metre	*The area enclosed by a square with sides of 1 metre long.*
Square shape	*Shape of face suited by softer hair style and jaw line partially covered.*
Stainless steel	*A very durable metal.*
Stance	*The way you stand.*
Standard form	*Used so that very large or very small numbers can be written in a more convenient way.*
Standards moderation	*The means by which awarding bodies ensure consistency across centres and ensure that national standards are being maintained and applied.*
State	*To express.*
Stationery	*Paper and office materials.*
Statistics	*Numerical data.*
Sterile	*Free from disease-causing micro-organisms.*

Sterling	*Currency of the UK.*
Stimulate	*To provoke or cause feeling.*
Stock	*Products held in the salon for sale or treatment.*
Stopcock	*A valve that opens and closes a gas or water supply pipe.*
Straight pins	*Strong pins used for long hairstyles and holding rollers.*
Straighteners	*Electrical device used to straighten hair.*
Straightening	*Method used to make curly hair straight.*
Straightening irons	*Electrical device used to straighten hair.*
Strand	*Term used for small group of hairs.*
Strand test	*Test used to monitor colour development.*
Strength	*Something that is done well.*
Stretch	*Test used to measure the tensile strength of hair.*
Structure	*A build-up of parts.*
Sturdy	*Strong.*
Subdivide	*To divide something that has already been divided.*
Substantive	*A thing or idea.*
Sulphur	*Main chemical of the amino acid cysteine.*
Sunlight	*Natural light rays that can damage hair.*
Supervisor	*The person in charge.*
Surface conditioner	*Work on the surface layer of the hair, coating the hair shaft and filling any gaps in the cuticle layer that have been caused by previous treatments.*
Surfactant	*Detergent that can damage the hair.*
Survey	*A method of collecting measured information.*
Symmetric	*To have equal distribution.*
Sympathetically	*To be sympathetic. To understand how someone may feel.*
Tactful	*To show skills in sensing the correct way to deal with others.*
Tail comb	*Used to help sectioning hair while setting.*
Tangled	*In a mess.*
Tapering	*Alternative term for 'feathering'.*
Target	*Objective set down for staff to reach.*
Target colour	*The hair colour chosen by the client.*
Team working	*A group of people working together.*
Technician	*A person who is trained in the technicalities (small details) of a subject.*
Technique	*A specific method of working.*
Telogen	*Stage of hair growth when follicles and papilla are in stage of rest.*
Temperature	*The heat level.*
Temporary	*Type of colour group (azo dyes).*
Tensile (strength)	*Ability of hair to be stretched.*
Tension	*Stretched.*
Terminal	*Hair of face, arms, pubic regions.*
Test curl	*Test to determine if full head can be permed.*
Test cut	*Test sample of hairs to assess the effect of colouring.*
Texture	*The coarseness or fineness of hair.*
Theme	*Subject matter.*
Thinning	*Reduce the volume of hair.*
Timeliness	*Reference to the time that information was recorded.*

Tinea capitis	*Fungal infection, contagious.*
Tinting	*Colouring with highlights or lowlights.*
Tinting cap	*Cap through which strands of hair are pulled to be tinted.*
Tolerance	*The amount that somebody can resist.*
Tone	*Warm or cool shade of colour tint.*
Toner	*Colour used to neutralise unwanted tones in lightened hair.*
Tool	*An implement used for working.*
Toxic	*Poisonous and harmful.*
Tracking	*The method by which a learner's achievements are recorded across a range of activities.*
Traction alopecia	*A condition in which the hair falls out due to excessive pulling.*
Trainee	*A person who is training for a particular job role.*
Training	*To learn skills.*
Transaction	*The agreement between a seller and buyer for a good or service.*
Transfer	*To move from one area to another.*
Translucent	*Has no colour.*
Treatment	*A service.*
Treatment conditioners	*Work by penetrating the cortex and help to repair damage by adding protein. They are known as substantive products.*
Trichologist	*A specialist in hair and scalp conditions.*
Trichorrhexis nodosa	*Small white nodules along the hair shaft.*
Twist	*A channel of hair that has been wound around itself.*
Twisting	*The method of twisting a channel of hair around itself.*
Ultraviolet	*Type of light ray; can be harmful.*
Unauthorised	*Not allowed.*
Under cut	*To remove hair under the baseline.*
Uniform	*To be evenly spaced.*
Uniform layer cut	*Both sides of the hair cut evenly.*
Upper quartile	*Data is split into 4 equal quarters. The highest quarter is referred to as the upper quartile. For example the upper quartile of 100 is the highest 25 of the numbers.*
Upward nape	*Hair grows upward from the nape.*
UV	*Ultraviolet. Type of light ray; can be harmful.*
VAT	*Value added tax.*
Vellus	*Fine body hair.*
Velocity	*The speed or rate of motion at which something is travelling.*
Vent brush	*Type of brush; creates a broken casual effect.*
Venue	*A place where an event is held.*
Verbal	*Any form of communication that uses words, e.g. speaking and writing in the form of letters, newspapers, emails etc.*
Vigorously	*Active strength.*
Virgin hair	*Hair that has not been chemically treated or bleached.*
Virus	*A tiny organism that causes infectious disease.*
VISA	*Credit card company.*
Vocabulary	*Words and their meanings.*
Volume	*Length x width x height.*
Warm shade	*Colour such as red or orange.*
Warts	*Caused by viral infection of epidermis: non-contagious if not damaged.*

Waste	*To throw away.*
Water soluble	*Dissolves in water.*
Water waving	*Another name for finger waving.*
Watermark	*A design that is visible when held up to the light.*
Wax	*A product used during styling and setting, usually made from beeswax.*
Weakness	*Tasks that need improvement in performance.*
Weave cutting	*Scissors 'snip' at roots; creates texture and strengthens root support.*
Weave foil	*Method of tinting hair by placing sections on foil.*
Weaving	*Interlacing hair.*
Web browser	*A software package that allows you to view pages from the World Wide Web. Examples are Internet Explorer and Netscape.*
Web page	*A document, usually written in HTML (Hypertext Mark-up Language), that can be accessed on the Internet.*
Website	*A collection of electronic 'pages'.*
Weight	*Distribution of hair length within a haircut.*
Wet shampoo	*Shampoo that requires water.*
Whorl	*A growth pattern that follows a circular shape.*
Widow's peak	*Growth pattern; hairline points in middle of forehead.*
Winding	*Technique to change the shape of hair.*
Word processor	*A computer program used to create text based documents such as letters and memos, although graphics may also be added.*
World Wide Web	*The WWW is a collection of electronic 'pages' that can be accessed over the Internet. The World Wide Web is NOT the same as the Internet; it is only a part of it.*
Woven hair	*Interlacing hair to other pieces of hair or other items.*
Wrapping lotion	*The product used in the second step of a two-step perm.*
Zinc pyrithione	*Chemical in shampoo that lifts off top layer dead skin cells.*

Index

Numbers in **bold** indicate figures and tables